TADAO ANDO RECENT PROJECT 3

Edited by Yoshio Futagawa

Copyright ©2021 A.D.A. EDITA Tokyo Co., Ltd.
3-12-14 Sendagaya, Shibuya-ku, Tokyo 151-0051, Japan
All rights reserved. No part of this publication may be reproduced,
stored in a retrieval system, or transmitted,
in any form or by any means, electronic, mechanical,
photocopying, recording, or otherwise,
without permission in writing from the publisher.

Copyright of photographs
©2021 GA photographers
Copyright of drawings, renderings
©2021 Tadao Ando Architect & Associates

Printed and bound in Japan

ISBN 978-4-87140-693-2 C1052

TADAO ANDO
RECENT PROJECT 3

A.D.A. EDITA Tokyo

RECENT
PROJECT 3

TADAO

ANDO

TADAO ANDO RECENT PROJECT 3
CONTENTS

ESSAY

ARCHITECTURE AS "JEWEL BOX" TO STIMULATE THE CITY
Tadao Ando

都市を刺激する〈宝石箱〉としての建築
安藤忠雄

At the western end of the Les Halles district of Paris, *the Bourse de Commerce* has existed quietly through the tumultuous centuries of the historical city. A project to transform this historic building into a contemporary art museum has finally reached completion. It was opened at last, COVID-19 pandemic permitting.

The project involved a challenging construction of erecting a cylinder space finished with raw concrete inside the central rotunda. Boldly inserting a new space into an old structure, creating a dialogue between the new and the old, and breathing new life into the space; the concept is the extension of that of *the Punta della Dogana* in Venice.

The client for both projects, from Venice to Paris, is François Pinault. In fact, my first project with Mr. Pinault was *the François Pinault Foundation for Contemporary Art* on the Île Seguin in Paris in the early 2000s. It was discontinued for various reasons, which in turn led to a series of projects in Venice, and then a second challenge back in Paris.

Under unique site conditions on Île Seguin, we focused our energy on the theme of inheritance of urban memory. The results of this exploration have been transformed and utilized in the current project. What is more, the starting point of the series of conversion projects with was *the Nakanoshima Project II (Urban Egg)*, which was conceived in the 1980s. It was a project to revitalize a public hall in my hometown Osaka, which I created without being commissioned by anyone. Because it was an independent proposal, I put a lot of effort into the drawings and poured my energy into the model. In the end, the city authorities did not take me seriously, and I ended up simply adding it to my list of unbuilt projects, but I had always carried the ideas that I discovered there close to my heart. Thus, the central court at *the Punta della Dogana* was the fruit of two decades of work, and the cylinder space at *the Bourse de Commerce* was the new challenge I took on after three decades.

Every architecture is created under different conditions, from the surrounding environment to the program, or the client's personality. By making the most of these dif-

パリ・レアール地区の西端で，激動する歴史都市の数世紀を静かに生き続けてきた「ブルス・ドゥ・コメルス」。この歴史的建造物を現代美術館に再生するプロジェクトがついに完成，コロナ禍を経てオープンを迎えた。

中央のロトンダに，打放しコンクリートによるシリンダー空間を立ち上げるという難工事だった。旧い建物の内側に新たな空間を大胆に挿入し，そこに喚起される新旧の対話で場に生命を吹き込む——このコンセプトは，先にヴェニスでつくった「プンタ・デラ・ドガーナ」の延長線上にあるものだ。

ヴェニスからパリ，いずれのプロジェクトもクライアントはフランソワ・ピノー氏である。実は，ピノー氏との最初の仕事は2000年代初めに，パリ，スガン島に計画した「ピノー現代美術館」だった。それが諸事情で中断されたがために，ヴェニスでの一連のプロジェクトが生まれ，そして，パリへの二度目の挑戦が始まったというわけだ。

スガン島では，特殊な立地状況のもと，都市の記憶の継承というテーマの追及にエネルギーを注いだ。そのスタディの成果が，形を変え，今の計画に生きている。さらに言えば，一連の入れ子構造による改造プロジェクトの原点にあるのは，1980年代に企てた「中之島プロジェクトII（アーバンエッグ）」である。

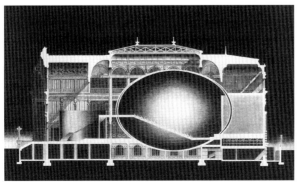

Urban Egg (Nakanoshima Project II)

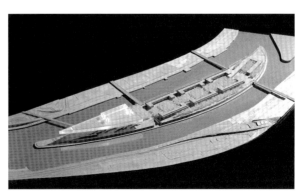

François Pinault Foundation for Contemporary Art

Punta della Dogana Renovation

ferences, we create a place that can only be created there. In every job, a different architectural story is born.

Sometimes, over time, the story takes an unexpected turn. Such is the case with the aforementioned two-city project with François Pinault; or the three-decade-long work with Soichiro Fukutake at Naoshima Island which began at the end of the 1980s and has resulted in seven buildings, two of which are currently under construction. An ongoing project to extend *the Kröller-Müller Museum* in the Netherlands, known for the "Van Gogh Forest," is also part of a grand history that began back in the time of Henry van de Velde. By "creating" again on a particular "site" with existing components, a new future unfolds for a story. While extensions and renovations have certain limitations, they are more than compensated for by the creative possibilities that it holds within.

It is not only public museums that have unique stories to tell. I have come to be involved in many never-ending stories of architecture. One is *the Rock Field Shizuoka Factory*, a food factory project that has been built over four phases since the 1990s with the concept to create a place where employees could first and foremost spend their time in comfort. Another is the campus project for *the International Pacific University*, where five buildings have been built intermittently over the past 15 years under the theme of "forest of learning."

Architecture is an act of expression, but after all, it is a social and economic activity. No matter how inventive the architects are, nothing will happen without the opportunities to flourish. In this sense, it is the client who is indeed the driving force in bearing architecture, considering who prepares the land and the funds scheming a new building. In fact, behind every unique piece of architecture, there is always a glimpse of an equally person who has a lot of personality, such as Edgar Kaufmann for F. L. Wright's *Fallingwater*, or Eusebi Güell for Antoni Gaudí's *Park Güell*.

In each of the projects mentioned above, the client is the protagonist. As with *the Bourse de Commerce, the He Art Museum* in Guangdong, China which opened this year, was also a project with a client who had solid

誰に頼まれたわけでもなく，地元大阪のパブリック・ホールの再生を目指したプロジェクトだ。自主提案だからこそ，ドローイングに力を込め，模型にエネルギーを注いだ。結局，市当局には相手にされず，単にアンビルトの記録を増やすに終わったが，ここで発見したアイディアをずっと胸の内に抱えてきた。それが20年越しに実ったのが，「プンタ・デラ・ドガーナ」のセントラルコートであり，30年越しの，そのまた新たな挑戦が今回の「ブルス・ドゥ・コメルス」のシリンダー空間であった。

建築とは周辺環境からプログラム，クライアントの個性など，すべて異なる与条件の下につくられるものだ。その差異を生かし，味方につけることで，そこにしかできない場をつくる。全ての仕事に，異なる建築の物語が生まれる。

その物語が，時の流れの中で，ときに思いもよらぬ展開を見せることがある。前述のフランソワ・ピノー氏との二都市にまたがるプロジェクト，あるいは，1980年代末に始まり，今日までに七つの建物を完成し，二つが現在進行中の直島，福武總一郎さんとの30年越しの仕事などは正にそれだ。現在進行中のオランダ，〈ゴッホの森〉で知られるクレラー・ミュラー美術館の増築プロジェクトもまた，アンリ・ヴァン・デ・ヴェルデらの時代に始まる壮大な歴史の一端を担うものだ。既存部分を含めた特別な〈敷地〉に，もう一度〈つくる〉ことで物語の新たな未来が始まる。増改築には一定の制限がある一方で，それを補って余りある，創造的可能性が潜んでいる。

ユニークな物語を持つのは，パブリックの美術館ばかりではない。「何よりもそこで働く従業員が快適に時を過ごせる場所を」とのコンセプトから，環境づくりをテーマに1990年代から四期にわたる増築を経て緑あふれるファクトリー・パークを実現した食品工場プロジェクト「ロック・フィールド静岡ファクトリー」や，〈学びの森〉をコンセプトに15年間余りをかけて五棟の校舎を断続的に建設している「IPU・環太平洋大学」のキャンパス計画など，気が付けば終わらない建築の物語にいくつも参加させてもらっている。

建築は表現行為である一方で，あくまで社会的な，経済行為だ。建築家がいかに創意を燃やそうとも，それを開花させる機会がなければ，何も始まらない。その意味では，土地と資金を準備して新たな建築を構想するクライアントこそが，建築を

ambition. The project was by a Chinese electrical manufacturer giant Midea Group, and it was established right next to their office building. Without being hindered by the pandemic of the past year, the museum has opened with ambitious exhibitions. We can sense the cultural maturity of China and look forward to a great development of this story after the completion of the building.

Reflecting on my works, I am once again reminded of the fact that I have been blessed with clients. At the same time, I realize that each of my projects has been deeply influenced by "the city," the context of the site in which it was built. What I am trying to talk about here is not about any theme of urban landscape, but the traces of human lives through time quietly imprinted into the landscape like a stratum. I am talking about "the city" as the very substance of human history that has been cultivated in that place.

New architecture must start from a dialogue with history, and respond to the physical, living, and cultural context that has nurtured the landscape. However, the response does not have to be for harmony nor conformance. It can be a courageous dialogue that accepts the existing context but dares to insert a foreign object that conflicts with it, creating a new context through its stimulus. *Grands Projets* of Paris in the late 20th century, starting with *the Centre Pompidou* and ending with *Le Grand Louvre*, established such ideology in architectural culture.

What is interesting, is that the greatness of the influence does not depend on the scale of the project. It was demonstrated by the modest yet significant shop designs by architect Hans Hollein in the 1960s in the ancient city of Vienna.

In short, what is needed is a critical attitude towards an existing city, implemented through architecture. The more essential the criticism, and the more radical its expression, the more it confronts the existing urban and social systems. The result is a powerful and beautiful "jewel box" of architecture, a network of dots embedded in the town, which breathes life into the city.

The true value of a "jewel box" is not in the

産み出す力の根幹だといえるだろう。実際，F・L・ライト設計の「落水荘」のエドガー・カウフマンしかり，アントニオ・ガウディ設計の「グエル公園」のエウセビ・グエルしかり，個性的な建築の背後には，必ず同じくらい強烈な人物の影が見え隠れする。

上述の，プロジェクトの数々も，いずれも主役はクライアントだ。「ブルス・ドゥ・コメルス」と同じく，今年オープンを迎えた中国広州の「和美術館」も同じく，確かな志を持ったクライアントとの仕事だった。中国の家電大手の美的集団によって，彼らの自社オフィス棟に隣り合って設立されたものだが，昨年からのコロナ禍に呑まれることなく，意欲的な運営企画が始められている。中国の文化的成熟を感じるとともに，建物完成後の物語の大いなる展開が期待される。

こうして自らの仕事を振り返ると，改めて「クライアントに恵まれた」という事実を痛感すると同時に，その一つひとつが，それが建つ場所の文脈，すなわち〈都市〉に色濃く影響を受けていることに気づく。ここで言いたいのは，都市景観といったテーマではない。その風景に，ひっそりと地層のように刻まれている，時代時代の人々の生きた痕跡。その場所で培われて

きた人間の歴史の実体そのものとしての〈都市〉の話だ。

新たな建築は，その歴史との対話を出発点として，その場所の風景を育んだ物理的，生活的，文化的文脈への応答としてつくられてしかるべきである。だがその応答は，必ずしも調和，適合を図るものでなくともよいだろう。既存の文脈を受け止めた上で，あえてそれと軋轢を起こすような異物を挿入，その刺激によって新たな文脈をつくりだすというような，勇敢な対話もありうる。「ポンピドゥー・センター」に始まり，「グラン・ルーヴル」へと至った，20世紀後半のパリの「グラン・プロジェ」などが，こうしたイデオロギーを建築文化として定着させた。

興味深いのは，その影響力の大小が，プロジェクトの規模の大小によるわけではないということだ。1960年代，古都ウィーンで，建築家ハンス・ホラインが展開したささやかな，しかし存在感のある店舗のデザインが，それを証明した。

要するに，必要なのは既存の都市に対する批判精神とその実践としての建築である。その批判が本質的であるほどに，その表現がラディカルであるほどに，既存の都市・社会制度と対立する。それを乗り越えて実現された，力強くも美しい〈宝石箱〉のような建築，街に埋め込まれたその〈宝石箱〉

Aerial view of Paris from east:
Bourse de Commerce / Pinault Collection
on right below

design of the box itself, but in how brightly it presents the "jewels" it contains, and how it can encourage the people who live in it to be active and creative. A city is not stimulated by a form, but by the radicalness of the public nature of the space.

The Nakanoshima Children's Book Forest, which I planned, built, and donated to the public in the spring of 2020, is my own attempt to create a "jewel box" of architecture.

The idea for this project came about when I was contemplating what I could do to repay Osaka in my own way, to the city that has raised me for half a century. If I were to create something, I wanted it to nurture the future of society, and I came up with the idea of a library for children. In this age of digitalization and multimedia, where we have become accustomed to the convenience of the information environment, I want to provide children with *inconvenient* paper books. The idea was to create an architectural space where children could encounter books in a free atmosphere as if they were exploring a forest.

In the completed "Book Forest," in a jungle gym-like reading room with a three-dimensional maze of stairs in a one-room space of three-story atrium, children find their favorite books and read them in their own way, in their own place, in their own style. "Humanity is capable of living a much more vigorous lifestyle." "There is work that architecture should do, that only architecture can do, to realize such a world." When I observe such scenes, I am greatly encouraged as these thoughts cross my mind.

The same project is now being carried out in Kobe, my other hometown, and also in Tono City, Iwate Prefecture, known for the "Folk Legends of Tono." We have just completed *the Tono Children's Book Forest* last month (July 2021).

Architecture cannot solve social problems, nor can it save souls. As I get older, the more I feel helpless, but at the very least, I can create opportunities for the children of the future to find their dreams through culture. I am willing to do as much as I can for as far as I can reach—with that in mind, I continue to work.

による点のネットワークが，都市に生命を吹き込む。

〈宝石箱〉の真価は，その箱自体のデザインの是非ではなく，それが内包する〈宝石〉をいかに輝かしく見せられるか，その空間を通じていかに活発で創造的な人々の活動を喚起できるか，によって決まるだろう。都市を刺激するのは，形ではない，その空間の公共的性格のラディカルさである。

2020年春，自ら企画立案して，建物をつくり，それをパブリックに寄付するという形で実現した「こども本の森 中之島」は，私なりに試みたこの〈宝石箱〉としての建築である。

構想のきっかけは「今日まで半世紀間，自分を育ててくれた大阪に，何か自分なりの恩返しができないか」と考えたことだった。つくるならば社会の未来を育てるものでありたいと考え，子どものための図書施設の計画に行き着いた。あらゆるメディアがデジタル化の波に呑み込まれ，マルチメディアと言われるような，便利な情報環境が日常化している今だからこそ，〈不便〉な紙の本を子どもたちに届けたい。その本と，森を探検するような自由な気分で子どもたちが出会える場所

を，建築でつくろうと考えた。

完成した〈本の森〉の，三層吹抜けのワンルームの空間に立体迷路のごとく階段が巡る，ジャングルジムのような閲覧室で，子どもたちはそれぞれに気に入った本を見つけ，思い思いの場所で，思い思いの格好で夢中になって読んでいる。そんな情景を眺めていると，「人間とはもっともっと逞しく生きられる存在なのだ」，「そんな世界の実現のために，建築がやるべき，建築にしかできない仕事があるのだ」と，大いに励まされる。

同じ企画を私のもう一つの故郷である神戸市，さらに縁あって，『遠野物語』で知られる岩手県の遠野市でも試みることとなり，先に，地元の民家を利用した「こども本の森 遠野」がつい先月（2021年7月）完成した。

建築で，社会問題を解決できるわけでもなければ，人の魂を救えるわけでもない。年を重ねるにつれ，無力を痛感するが，それでも，文化を拠り所に，明日を担う子どもたちがそれぞれの夢を見出すきっかけづくりくらいできるだろう。自分の手の届く精一杯のところで，やれるだけのことをしていきたい。そんな思いを胸に，仕事を続けている。

TADAO ANDO
RECENT PROJECT

Bourse de Commerce / Pinault Collection
ブルス・ドゥ・コメルス／ピノー・コレクション

Paris, France
フランス, パリ
2016-21

View from west toward entrance
西よりエントランス方向を見る

Entrance エントランス

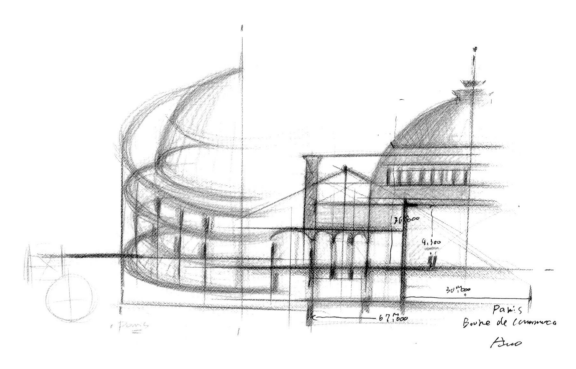

Inserted new windbreak room　挿入された新たな風除室

Rotunda　ロトンダ

Located in the heart of Paris, *the Bourse de Commerce* is an extension and renovation of a former grain exchange into a contemporary art museum. The first project with the client, François Pinault, was *the Pinault Museum of Contemporary Art* on the island of Seguin in Paris, which was selected in an international competition in the 2000s. Mr. Pinault expressed his dream of creating a museum that combines the characteristics of a Gothic cathedral and a Romanesque chapel, with a dignified appearance and a tranquil, introspective space adjacent to the origin of French industry and a sacred place for the labour movement. I fought the competition, elated by the stimulating program. After I was lucky enough to win, I kept the momentum going toward the realization of the project. However, there are many difficulties in a large-scale project. Four years after the competition, the project was cancelled due to problems with the urban infrastructure. It was just about the time to begin construction, when the construction documents were completed, and the demolition of the existing buildings was finished.

It was then the series of project in Venice began successively after the project in Paris. The project began with *Palazzo Grassi* (2006), then *Punta della Dogana* (2009), and *Teatrino* (2013). In a little over 9 years, we designed two museums and a theater along the Grand Canal. It was an extremely dynamic and exciting process, but the "dream" of a museum in Paris must have remained alive in Pinault's mind. Such was the story behind this project.

The original structure of *the Bourse de Commerce* was built for its main part at the end of the 18th century as the Halle au Ble. Then at the end of the 19th century, it became *the Bourse de Commerce* by Henri Blondel's renovation and conversion. Respecting the memory of the city contained in its old walls of the building, I made a plan to embed a new space inside the building and transform its entire interior into an exhibition space for contemporary arts. The goal shall be a

Entry of rotunda　ロトンダの入口

space connecting the past with the present and future.

Bourse de Commerce was originally a circular plan and has a symbolic rotunda in the middle of the site. I placed a concrete cylinder, 29 m in diameter and 9 m in height, in the building as an interior structure. This produced the main exhibition space, which has a sense of centripetal force, under the cupola, and an auditorium is included in the basement. The cylinder also had a cloistered space with the facade by Blondel. This passage-like space,

which has a hallway and a staircase along the circular wall, is the circulation zone for access to the triple-layer exhibition spaces and the auditorium in the basement.

The client once described to me his ideal museum like this, "It should have an architecture that possesses a tranquil self-reflective space full of a majestic atmosphere, as it conveys the sense of both a Gothic cathedral and a Romanesque chapel". I hope that this museum will become part of the scenery of Paris; a place where the people's heart is.

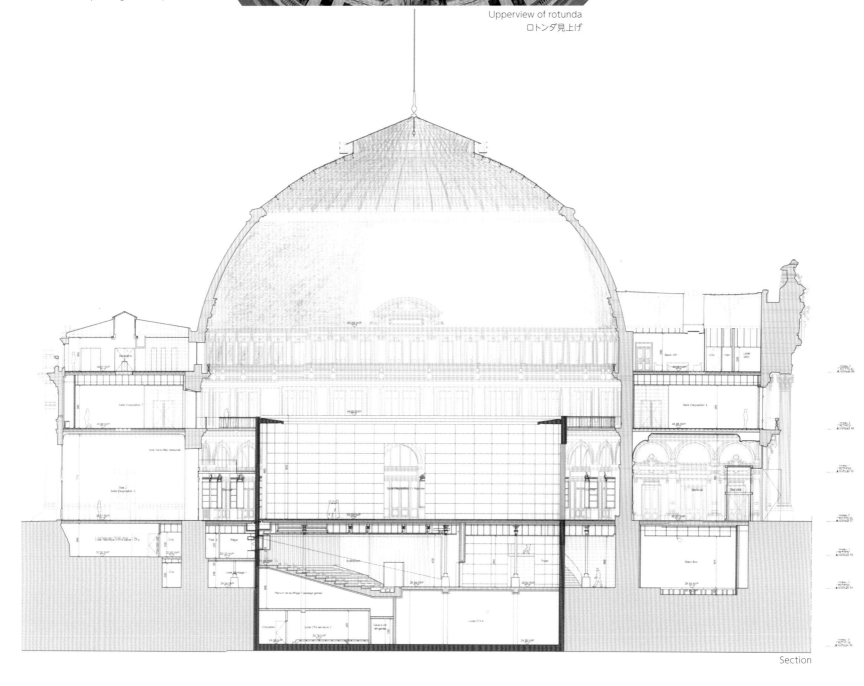

Upperview of rotunda
ロトンダ見上げ

Section

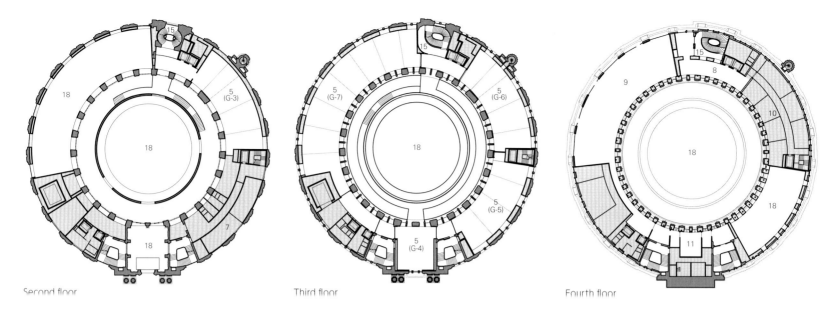

Second floor

Third floor

Fourth floor

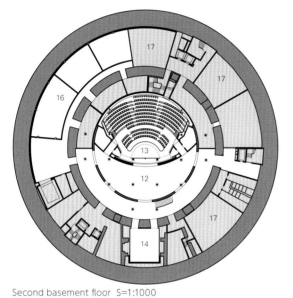

Second basement floor S=1:1000

First floor

1   ENTRANCE
2   ROTUNDA
3   ENTRANCE LOBBY
4   BOOK SHOP
5   GALLERY
6   LOADING
7   ATELIER
8   LOUNGE
9   RESTAURANT
10 OFFICE
11 VIP LOUNGE
12 FOYER
13 AUDITORIUM
14 BLACK BOX GALLERY
15 HISTRICAL STAIRCASE
16 PREPARATION ROOM
17 MECHANICAL
18 VOID

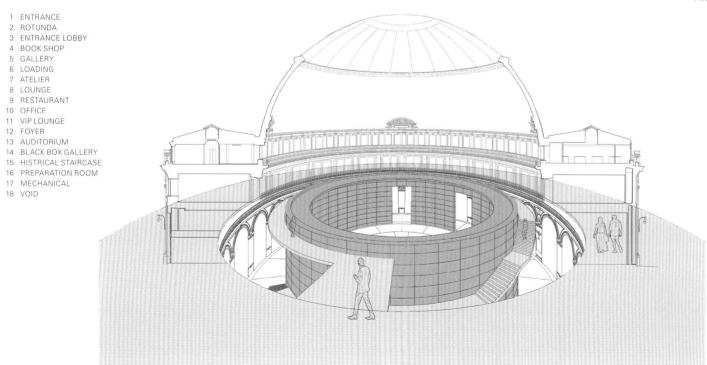

Perspective

パリ中心部に建つ歴史的建造物ブルス・ドゥ・コメルスを現代美術館として再生した計画である。クライアントであるフランソワ・ピノー氏との最初の仕事は，2000年に国際コンペで選ばれた，パリ，スガン島の「ピノー現代美術館」だった。フランス産業揺籃の地にして，労働運動の聖地ともなった敷地を前に，氏は「威厳ある佇まいを持ちながら，静謐で内省的な空間を湛える，ゴシックの大聖堂とロマネスクの礼拝堂の性質を兼ね備えた美術館をつくりたい」と夢を語っていた。私も刺激的なプログラムに高揚しながらコンペを闘い，運よく勝利した後も，そのままの勢いで実現に向け邁進した。だがビッグ・プロジェクトが故の難しさである。コンペから4年を経て，実施設計が完了，既存建物解体も終わり着工まであと一歩というところで，都市インフラ整備の問題で計画は中止となった。

　そして場所を変え，新たにスタートしたのが，ヴェネツィアの一連のプロジェクトだった。「パラッツォ・グラッシ」(2006年)からスタートして，「プンタ・デラ・ドガーナ」(2009年)，「テアトリーノ」(2013年)と9年余りの間に，大運河でつながる二つの美術館と一つの劇場をつくった。それは極めてダイナミック，エキサイティングなプロセスであったが，ピノー氏の心の中には，パリの美術館という〈夢〉は変わらず生き続けていたのだろう。そんな物語が，今回のプロジェクトの背後にはあった。

　「ブルス・ドゥ・コメルス」は，その主要部が18世紀後半に穀物取引所として建てられ，その後19世紀末のアンリ・ブロンデルによる改修により「ブルス・ドゥ・コメルス」として現在の形となった。その壁に刻まれた都市の記憶に敬意を払いつつ，その内側に新たな空間を入れ子構造として挿入することで，内部空間全体を現代美術のための空間として再生する——主題は過去から現代，未来へと時間をつなぐ建築である。

　建物は，円形平面で中央に象徴的なロトンダ空間を持つ。そこに，高さ約9mのコンクリートの壁で囲われた，直径29mのシリンダーを挿入することで，内部空間を再構成する。これにより，クーポラ(ドーム天井)の下に，求心力ある展示空間が生まれ，さらにその地下部分にオーディトリアムが内包される。シリンダーはまた，その外側に，ブロンデルによるファサードと対峙する新たな回廊空間をつくりだす。円形の壁に沿って通路，階段が巡る，このパッサージュが，ロトンダを取り巻く三層の展

Entry of rotunda　ロトンダの入口

29

Rotunda on left, passage on right　左にロトンダ, 右に回廊

示エリアや地階のオーディトリアムにアクセスするためのサーキュレーション・ゾーンとなる。

かつて，クライアントは，彼にとっての理想の美術館のイメージを「威厳ある佇まいを持ちながら静謐で内省的な空間を湛える，ゴシックの大聖堂とロマネスクの礼拝堂の性質を兼ね備えた建築」という言葉で表現した。この美術館が，そのような，人々の心の拠り所となる建物としてパリの街に息づいていくことを期待している。

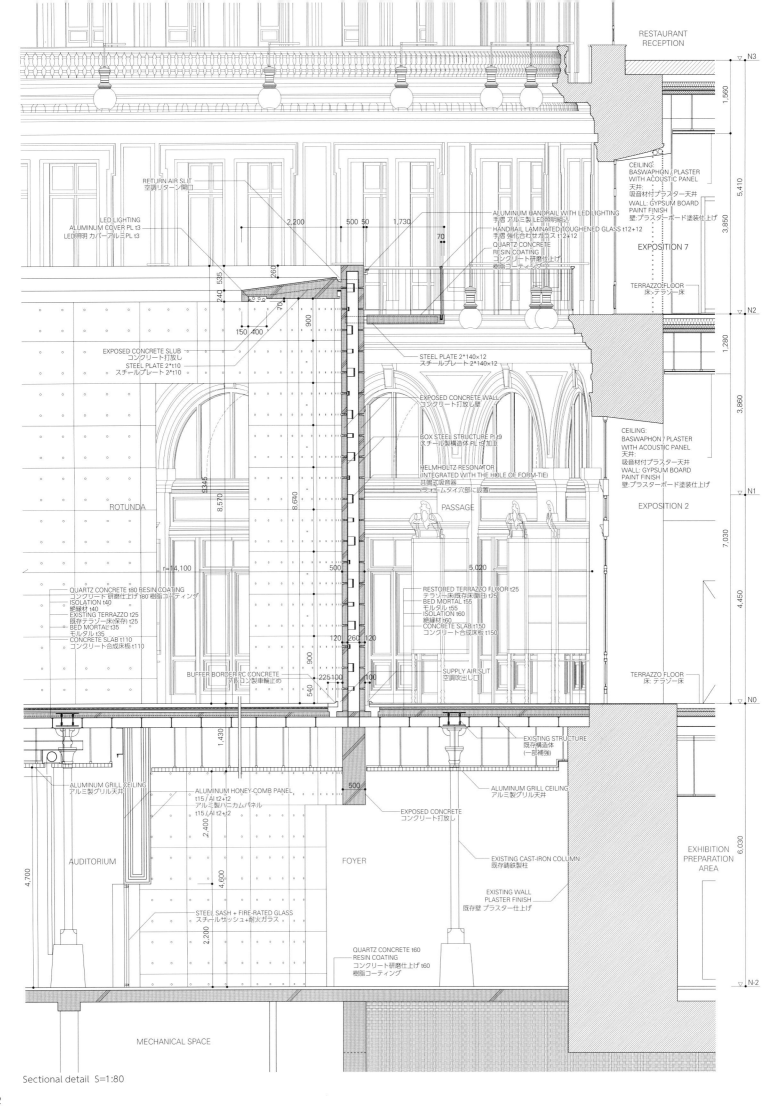

RESTAURANT
RECEPTION

N3

1,560

CEILING:
BASWAPHON / PLASTER
WITH ACOUSTIC PANEL
天井:
吸音材付プラスター天井
WALL: GYPSUM BOARD
PAINT FINISH
壁:プラスターボード塗装仕上げ

5,410

EXPOSITION 7

3,850

RETURN AIR SLIT
空調リターン開口

LED LIGHTING
ALUMINUM COVER PL t3
LED照明 カバーアルミPL t3

ALUMINUM HANDRAIL WITH LED LIGHTING
手摺 アルミ製 LED照明組込
HANDRAIL LAMINATED TOUGHENED GLASS t12+12
手摺 強化合わせガラス t12+12
QUARTZ CONCRETE
RESIN COATING
コンクリート研磨仕上げ
樹脂コーティング

2,200   500 50   1,730

70

TERRAZZO FLOOR
床:テラゾー床

N2

535
240   260
70
150   400   900

1,280

EXPOSED CONCRETE SLUB
コンクリート打放し
STEEL PLATE 2*t10
スチールプレート 2*t10

STEEL PLATE 2*140×12
スチールプレート 2*140×12

EXPOSED CONCRETE WALL
コンクリート打放し壁

BOX STEEL STRUCTURE PL t9
スチール製構造体 PL t9加工

HELMHOLTZ RESONATOR
(INTEGRATED WITH THE HOLE OF FORM-TIE)
共鳴式吸音器
(フォームタイ穴部に設置)

3,860

CEILING:
BASWAPHON / PLASTER
WITH ACOUSTIC PANEL
天井:
吸音材付プラスター天井
WALL: GYPSUM BOARD
PAINT FINISH
壁:プラスターボード塗装仕上げ

N1

9345
8,570   8,640

ROTUNDA

PASSAGE

EXPOSITION 2

7,030

r=14,100   500   5,020

QUARTZ CONCRETE t80 RESIN COATING
コンクリート研磨仕上げ t80 樹脂コーティング
ISOLATION t40
絶縁材 t40
EXISTING TERRAZZO t25
既存テラゾー床(保存) t25
BED MORTAL t35
モルタル t35
CONCRETE SLAB t110
コンクリート合成床板 t110

RESTORED TERRAZZO FLOOR t25
テラゾー床(既存床復旧) t25
BED MORTAL t55
モルタル t55
ISOLATION t60
絶縁材 t60
CONCRETE SLAB t150
コンクリート合成床板 t150

4,450

900
120 260 120

BUFFER BORDER PC CONCRETE
PC製コン製車輪止め
540   225 100   100

SUPPLY AIR SLIT
空調吹出し口

TERRAZZO FLOOR
床:テラゾー床

N0

1,430

EXISTING STRUCTURE
既存構造体
(一部補強)

ALUMINUM GRILL CEILING
アルミ製グリル天井

ALUMINUM HONEY-COMB PANEL
t15 / Al t2+2
アルミ製ハニカムパネル
t15 / Al t2+2

500

EXPOSED CONCRETE
コンクリート打放し

ALUMINUM GRILL CEILING
アルミ製グリル天井

EXISTING CAST-IRON COLUMN
既存鋳鉄製柱

EXHIBITION
PREPARATION
AREA

6,030

2,400

4,700   4,600

AUDITORIUM

FOYER

EXISTING WALL
PLASTER FINISH
既存壁 プラスター仕上げ

2,200

STEEL SASH + FIRE-RATED GLASS
スチールサッシ+耐火ガラス

QUARTZ CONCRETE t60
RESIN COATING
コンクリート研磨仕上げ t60
樹脂コーティング

N-2

MECHANICAL SPACE

Sectional detail S=1:80

32

Passage　回廊

Rotunda　ロトンダ

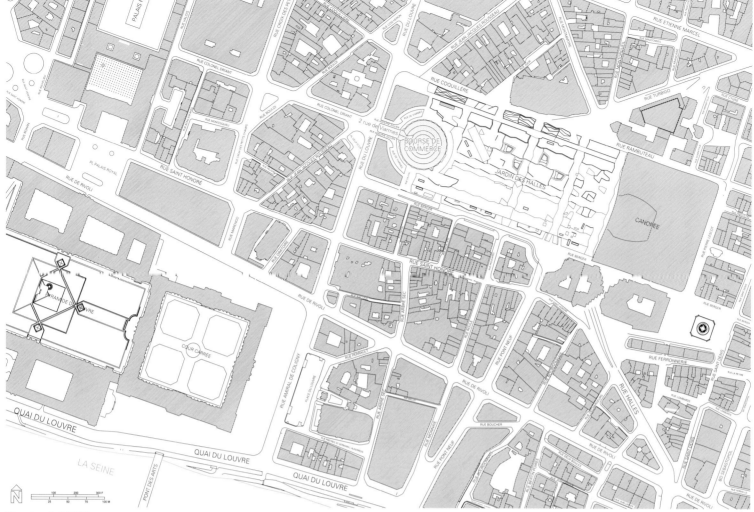

Site plan S=1:5000

Aerial view　鳥瞰全景

Passage　回廊

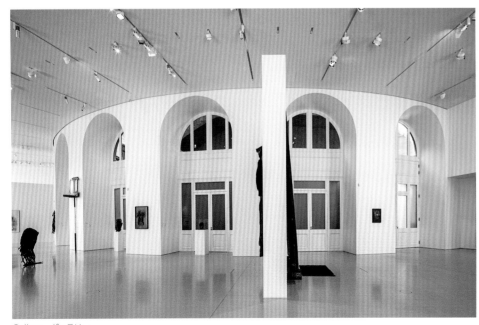

Gallery　ギャラリー

Entrance lobby　エントランスロビー

Exhibition room on second basement floor　地下2階展示室

Restored double spiral staircase at the time of construction
修復された建設当時の二重螺旋階段

Cloakroom

Corridor on second basement floor　地下2階通路

Auditorium on second basement floor　地下2階オーディトリアム

Foyer on second basement floor　地下2階ホワイエ

View from east side park　東側の公園より見る

Kröller–Müller Museum
クレラー・ミュラー美術館

Otterlo, the Netherlands
オランダ, オッテルロー
2018-

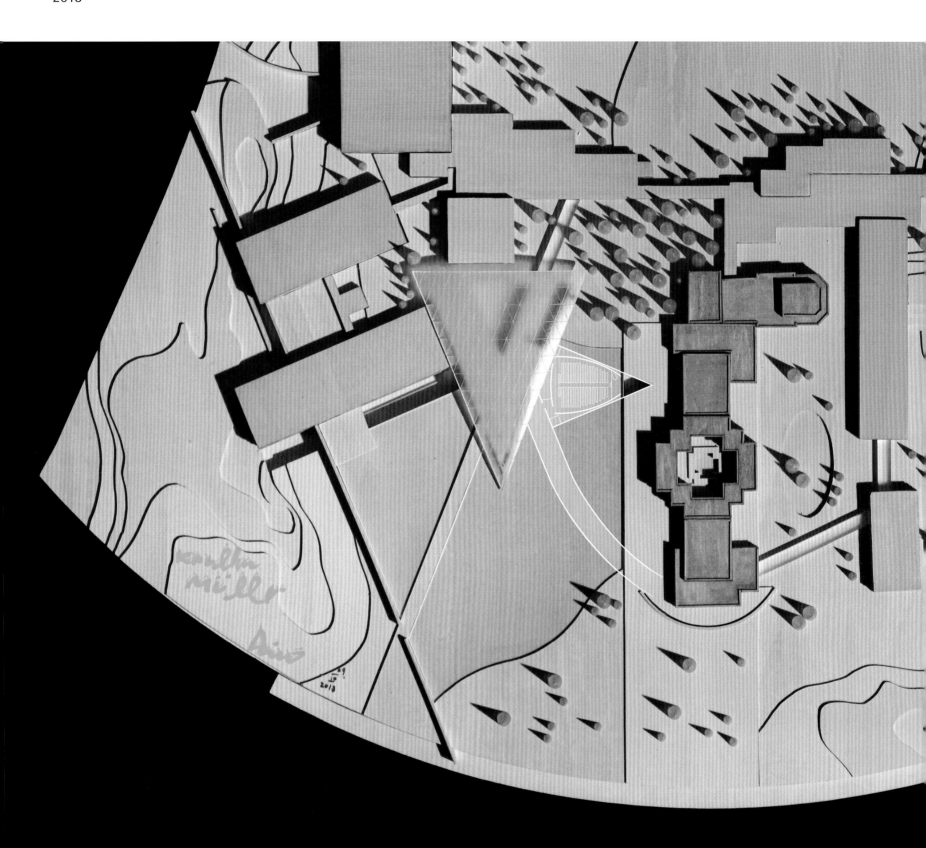

Site model　敷地模型

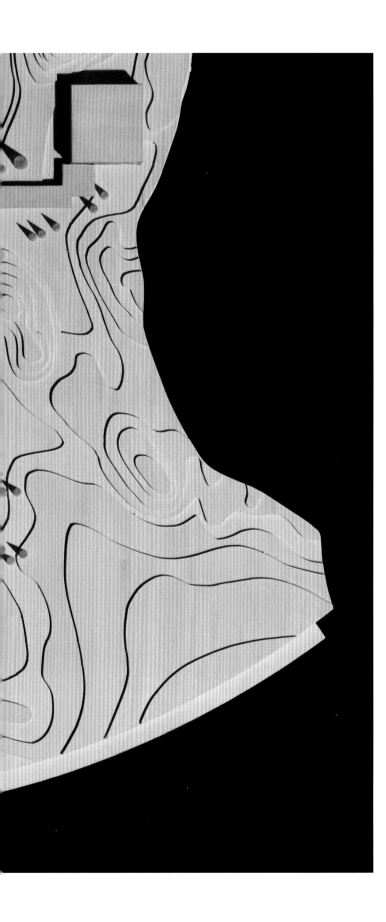

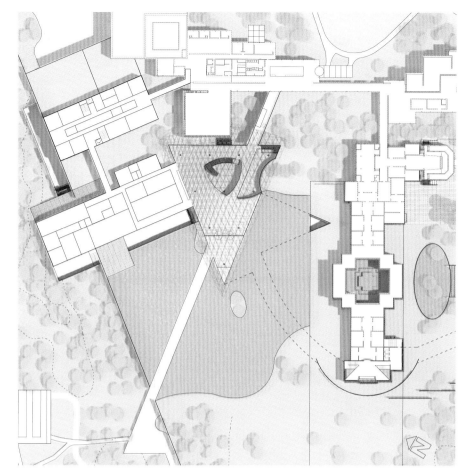

Site plan S=1:1800

Nestled in the Hoge Veluwe National Park in Otterlo, the Netherlands, the project is an extension to the existing *Kröller-Müller Museum*, renowned for its extensive sculpture garden and wide collection of paintings by Vincent van Gogh.

The museum was founded by art collector Helene Kröller-Müller. To realize her lifelong endeavor, she has engaged with Peter Behrens, Mies van der Rohe, and Hendrik Petrus Berlache prior to commissioning Henry van de Velde as the final architect for *the Kröller-Müller Museum*. The museum has continuously been expanded on since its opening in 1938. The sculpture garden was completed in 1961, succeeded by the completion of *Rietveld Pavilion* by Gerrit Rietveld in 1965, *the New Museum* by Wim Quist in 1970s, and *Aldo van Eyck Pavilion* in 2006. Over the decades, the museum has been gradually and intermittently growing. Today, the museum has matured into a place where art, nature, and architecture resonate in unison.

The newest intervention, to this relay of creation that transcends generations, must be created with two important objectives in mind. Firstly, the museum must be expanded to provide the necessary and sufficient functions while respecting the inherited spirit and the vernacular qualities that has nurtured it. Secondly, we must leave a contemporary intervention that responds to the architecture left by other predecessors.

The administration building, added in the 1970s, will be relocated to enhance the environment around the old building. Subsequently, a new volume will be placed while the preservation of the existing trees. The majority of the new extension will be submerged and will strengthen its ties with the landscape. The water feature in the entrance area will fuse the traditional and the contemporary.

As the visitors enter the approach to the museum, the glass roof will cast light on the entrance hall that leads to the basement, while reflecting the serene sky of Otterloo on its curved surface. This new experience will symbolize the next generation of *the Kröller-Müller Museum*.

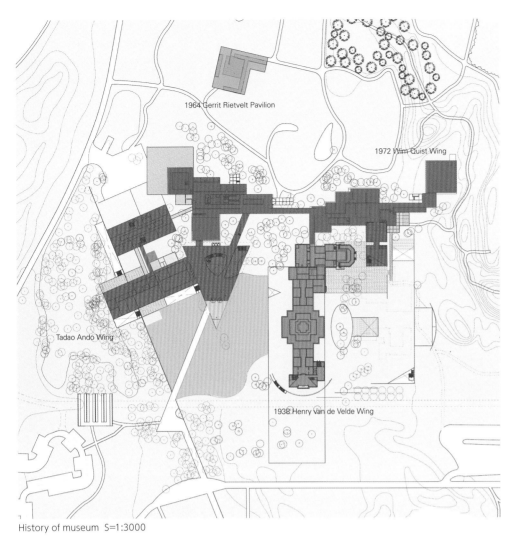

1964 Gerrit Rietvelt Pavilion

1972 Wim Quist Wing

Tadao Ando Wing

1938 Henry van de Velde Wing

History of museum S=1:3000

Proposals for
Kröller-Müller Museum
Above: Hendrik Petrus Berlage
Middle: Henry van de Velde
Below: Ludwig Mies van der Rohe

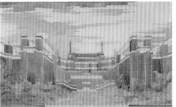

Site view　敷地鳥瞰

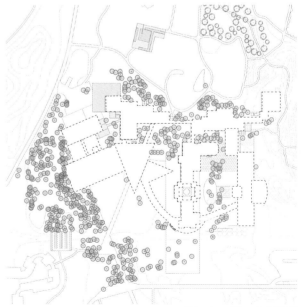

Wood position S=1:5000

Approach　アプローチ

敷地はオランダ オッテルローの, デ・ホーヘ・フェルウェ国立公園内に位置する。広大な彫刻庭園と, 世界屈指のゴッホのコレクションで知られる「クレラー・ミュラー美術館」の増築計画である。

　生涯をかけた事業として, ヘレン・クレラー・ミュラーは, ペーター・ベーレンス, ミース・ファン・デル・ローエ, ヘンドリク・ペトルス・ベルラーヘに検討を依頼したが, 最終的に, モダニズム黎明期の建築家アンリ・ヴァン・デ・ヴェルデの設計で1938年に開館した。その後, 戦争を挟んで, 61年に隣接する彫刻庭園が完成。続いて, 65年にリートフェルトのパヴィリオン, 70年代にウィム・

キストによる新館, 2006年にアルド・ファン・アイクのパヴィリオン……と, 数十年もの歳月をかけ, 生物が増殖するように, ゆっくりと断続的な拡張を重ねてきた。そして, 芸術と自然, 建築とが一体となって響き合う, 今日の美術館が生まれた。

　そんな世代を超えた創造のリレーに, 現代を生きる者の一人として参加する。受け継がれてきた精神, 育まれてきた場所の空気に敬意を払いつつ, 必要十分な機能的拡充を図ること。その上で, 先人達の残した空間に呼応するような現代の〈しるし〉を残すこと。この二点を主題に計画に臨んだ。

　まず, 70年代に加えられた管理棟を移設, 旧館周りの環境を整える。その上で, 既存の樹木を保護するように, 新たなヴォリュームを配置。その大部分は地下に沈め, よりランドスケープとの結びつきを強めた「クレラー・ミュラー美術館」を再構築する。エントランス・エリアに広がる水盤が新旧をつなぐ緩衝領域の役割を果たす。

　水上を伸びるアプローチ通路の先には, 地下へと続くエントランスホールの存在を暗示するガラス屋根が浮かび, 地下へと光を引き込みながら, その曲面にオッテルローの穏やかな空を映し出す。この水際の風景が, 次なる「クレラー・ミュラー美術館」を象徴する。

49

Entrance hall on basement　地階エントランスホール

Hall on basement　地階ホール

Entrance hall on ground level　1階エントランスホール

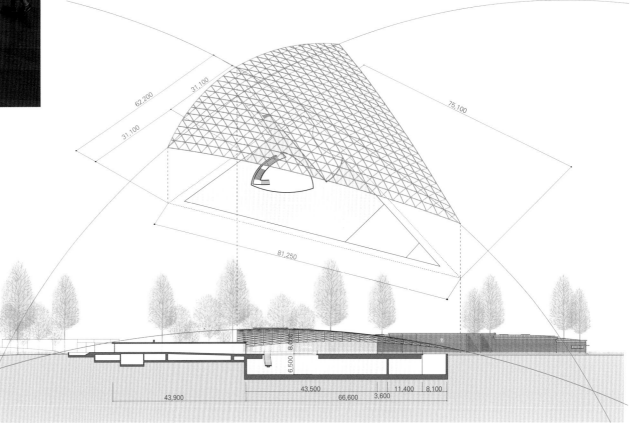

Section S=1:1200

Nakanoshima Children's Book Forest
こども本の森 中之島

Osaka, Osaka
大阪府大阪市
2017-19

View across Dojima-gawa river　堂島川越しに見る

View from southwest 南西より見る

Distant view from southeast　南東より見る遠景

Tadao Ando

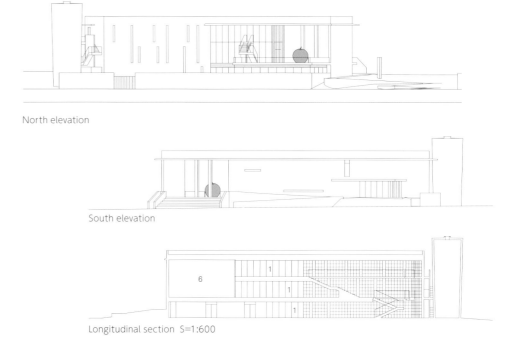

North elevation

South elevation

Longitudinal section　S=1:600

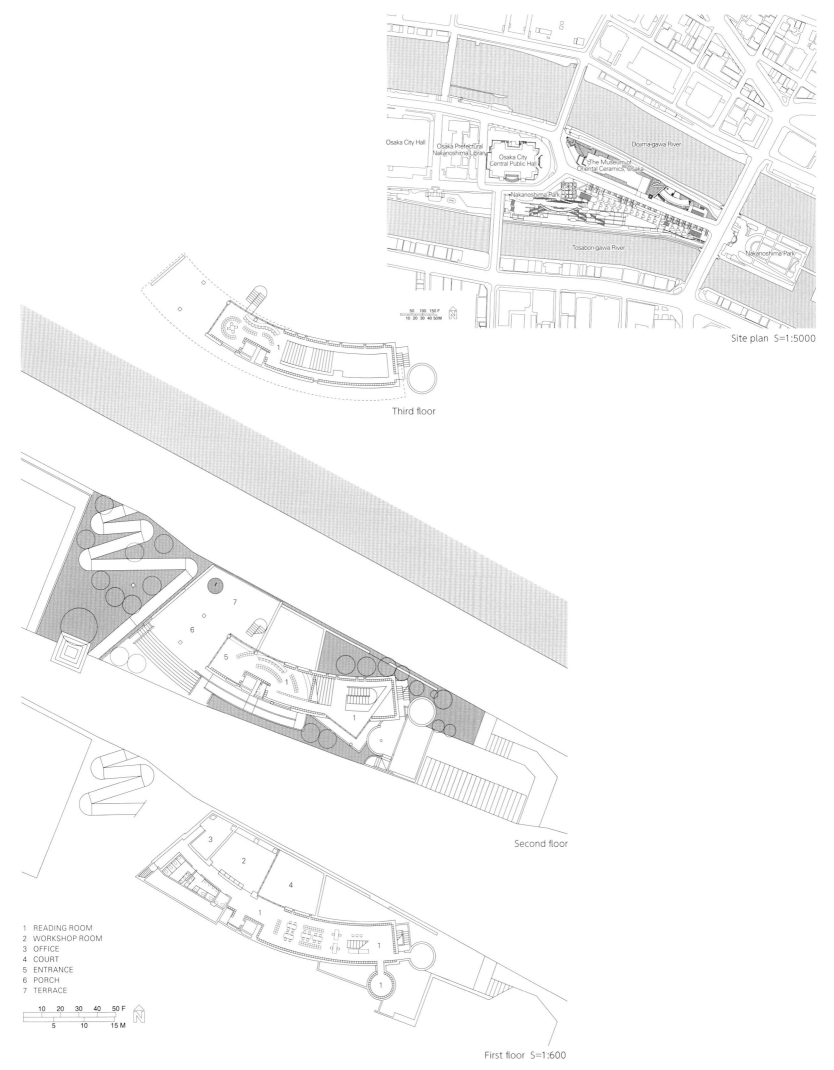

Site plan S=1:5000

Osaka City Hall
Osaka Prefectural
Nakanoshima Library
Osaka City
Central Public Hall
Dojima-gawa River
The Museum of
Oriental Ceramics, Osaka
Nakanoshima Park
Tosabori-gawa River
Nakanoshima Park

Third floor

Second floor

1 READING ROOM
2 WORKSHOP ROOM
3 OFFICE
4 COURT
5 ENTRANCE
6 PORCH
7 TERRACE

First floor S=1:600

57

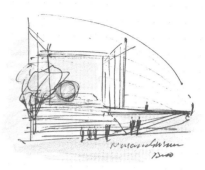

The Nakanoshima Children's Book Forest is a library where children can read, enjoy, and learn from the power of books. I collaborated with the city government of Osaka and planned this project to contribute to my hometown. I was born and raised in the Kansai area, and my entire career was established here. As a show of gratitude for my city, I decided to design and fund this structure by taking responsibility for the entirety of the project construction costs.

Nakanoshima is a slender island that lies between two rivers. The adjacent Dojima River crosses the north-south axis of the city, through an area of Osaka known as Mido-suji. Its crosshairs rest in the heart of the metropolis, a core of Osaka's history and culture. Every resident of Osaka understands the beauty of Nakanoshima and holds it dear to their heart. As a child, I frequented the landscape surrounding *the Nakanoshima Public Hall*, and it has stayed in my memories ever

◁ View from porch toward Dojima-gawa river. Entrance on right
ポーチより堂島川方向を見る。右にエントランス

since. In the late eighties, well after I had established my office, Nakanoshima made its way into my work. In a series of projects called *Urban Egg* and *Space Strata* I respectively proposed to insert a new "egg-shaped" auditorium in the public hall and developed a scheme for a spatially delightful underground complex. Though these projects were never realized, I believe it led to my current work to make Nakanoshima flourish.

I made other unsolicited project proposals in Nakanoshima that did not include designing new buildings. In 2004, I was able to successfully initiate a cherry tree planting initiative called the "Heisei-Era Alley of Cherry Blossoms." This campaign gathered the support of more than 50,000 local citizens. Collectively backing the goal of the world's longest and most beautiful row of cherry blossom trees is a testament to the proud public spirit of Osakans. In the past, Osaka citizens have pooled their finances to privately fund public projects such as bridges, roads, auditoriums, and renovations of the local castle. Nakanoshima Park is part of the landscape of Osaka and colors the tip of the island with a deep and verdant green. There could not be a more suitable site for a library for the children who will carry the future of Osaka to the next generation.

During the design process, I attempted to utilize the excellent geographical and historical context of the site. Above all, I prioritized how children would use the space. The building takes the shape of an arched bow extending along the Dojima River. The eastern side of the building is a raised waterfront terrace that connects to the building entrance. Immediately after entering the covered entrance of the building, visitors are welcomed by an enormous green apple sculpture known as *Youth*.

The interior of the building is com-

Reading room on second floor　2階閲覧室

posed of three stories surrounded by bookshelves, stairs, bridges, and passageways, much like a complex labyrinth of Piranesi. As visitors proceed through the "maze," the scenery of the Dojima River becomes wedged in the slivers between bookshelves. A mysterious projection overlooking the stairwell appears, where visitors can enjoy the transition of light through the day. Wandering through the library, children can find various and diverse reading spaces. When a child finds a book that piques their interest, they can read it wherever they please: on the stairs, inside a bookshelf nook, or at a reading room. If the weather is sunny, they can read outside surrounded by a view of nature and the river. Fortunately, the city government of Osaka recently decided to convert Nakanoshima-dori, the road immediately adjacent to the library, into a public plaza space. *The Children's Forest for Books* is a library where children can read freely. The activity of the library will radiate out of the building itself, encapsulating the whole of Nakanoshima Park.

The most vital part of this library was the gathering of yearly operating costs, which came from many donations from the private sector. Much like the "Heisei-Era Alley of Cherry Blossoms," many individuals and companies have been enthusiastic about contributing to this cause. *The Children's Book Forest* Nakanoshima aspires to create a space to educate children and illuminate the joy of reading and imagination. I wholeheartedly believe that this was a project supported by the overwhelming passion and power of Osaka.

Void of reading room　閲覧室の吹抜け

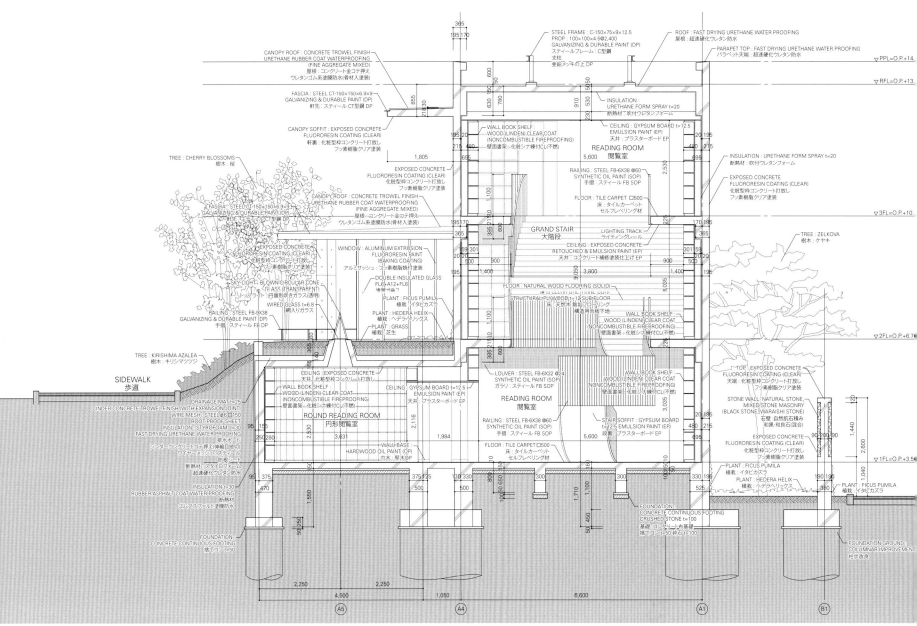

Sectional detail　S=1:100

私は生まれ育った大阪を拠点に活動を続けてきた。大阪に育てられた人間であり建築家である。その「恩返し」のつもりでこのプロジェクトを企画し，大阪市の協力を得て実現した。建設の費用は発案者である自身で責任を持った。

　敷地として市が選んだのは，中之島公園の一角。町を南北に長く貫く御堂筋に直交する川の中州，中之島は，大阪の歴史，文化の核として生き続けてきた，文字通りの街の心臓部だ。大阪人には特別な意味を持つ場所であり，私も小学校の写生で訪れたり，川にかかる銀橋のたもとで中学入学の記念写真を撮った。中之島公会堂を中心とする風景を，心の拠り所の一つとして育ってきた。1980年代に公会堂

を建て替え，一帯を再開発する計画が持ち上がった時は，既存建物を残すべく，頼まれもせず幾つもの再生計画を企てた。いずれも実現しなかったが，公会堂が残ったことは良かったと思う。

　2004年に始めた中之島を含む川沿いでの桜の植樹運動「桜の会・平成の通り抜け」は，5万人を超える市民の協力の下，植樹から維持管理まで確かな成果を残している。世界最長を目指すこの桜並木は，市民の力で橋を架け，道路を通し，公会堂を建て，城を再生してきた，大阪人の誇り高い公共精神の健在を証明するものだ。その後，武田五一設計の「銀橋」の拡張計画にも参加し，今回，その風景の一角を成す

中之島公園に大阪の未来を担う子どもたちのための建築「こども本の森」の敷地が得られた。これ以上相応しい敷地はないだろう。

　設計にあたっては，素晴らしい地理的，歴史的なコンテクストを十二分に活かすこと，何より子どもが主役であり，子どもが本と出会い，本を楽しみ，本に学ぶための施設であることを第一義に考えた。建物は，堂島川に沿って弓なりに伸びるヴォリューム形状で，東端に，エントランス・ポーチと連続して，子どもたちが川の風景に出会うテラスを設けた。ポーチを覆うゲートは，公園の緑と川をつなぎ，テラスでは「青春」と名付けられた大きな青リンゴのオブジェが訪れる子どもたちを出迎える。

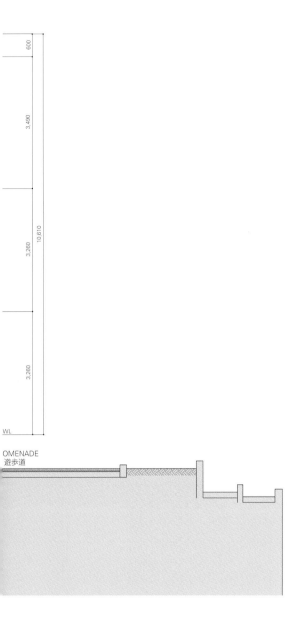

600

3.490

10.610

3.260

3.260

WL

OMENADE
遊歩道

Grand stairs on second floor　大階段

Cylindrical reading room on first floor　円筒形の閲覧室

　小さい建物だが，内部は壁という壁が本棚で覆い尽くされ，まるで本に包みこまれるような三層吹抜けの空間となっている。その中に階段やブリッジ通路を立体迷路のように巡らせた。ところどころに子どもが入り込める空間が散りばめられており，本棚のすき間から川の風景が目に飛び込んできたり，吹抜けを見下ろす飛び込み台のようなスペースが現れたり，明から暗へ一転，井戸の底のような円筒形の空間に行き当たったりする。その全てが子どものための閲覧室だ。気になる本が見つかったら，階段でもどこでも好きな場所で読み始めて構わない。天気が良ければ外に出て，水際テラスで本を開くこともできる。幸いにも，建物完成と前後して，公園の中央を通っていた中之島通りの歩行者空間化が決定した。子どもが自由に読書を楽しめる「本の森」が，公会堂や府立図書館もある公園一帯に広がった。

　蔵書の準備と運営資金では，「桜の会・平成の通り抜け」同様，民間に寄付を募り，多くの個人や企業が志を寄せてくれた。込められた人々の思いの分だけ建物は力強くまちに息づいていく。「こども本の森」もまた，大阪の民力が支えるプロジェクトであるが，未来に向けたこの運動は，神戸市や岩手県遠野市にも広がる予定である。

Bridge on second floor　2階ブリッジ

◁ Void of reading room: looking from grand stairs on third floor
3階大階段より閲覧室の吹抜けを見る

6 大阪→日本→世界 →

Osaka to Japan then to the World

Court on first floor　1階コート

Reading room on first floor: court on left　1階閲覧室。左にコート

Reading room on first floor　1階閲覧室

Reading room on first floor: cylindrical reading room inmost
1階閲覧室。奥に円筒状の閲覧室

◁ Downward view of void from third floor　3階より吹抜けを見下ろす

Entrance on second floor　2階エントランス

Infants corner on second floor　2階乳幼児コーナー

Entrance on second floor: looking toward porch
2階エントランス。ポーチ方向を見る

Reading room on third floor　3階閲覧室

Reading counter of entrance on second floor
2階エントランスの読書カウンター

Cylindrical room on first floor: images on wall projected to match the story of book
1階円筒空間。壁には本の物語に合わせた映像が投影される

Wrightwood 659
シカゴのギャラリー／Wrightwood 659

Chicago, U.S.A.
アメリカ合衆国, イリノイ州, シカゴ
2013-18

659

North elevation: *House in Chicago* by Tadao Ando in 1997 on right
北側立面。右に安藤によって1997年に建てられた「シカゴの住宅」

In 1997, we completed a project known as *the House in Chicago* near the center of the metropolitan area. This was our first building in the United States. Recently, the same client contacted us for a new architectural commission. The project involved the conversion of an ninety-year-old brick apartment into a contemporary art gallery adjacent to the home we had designed for him in the past.

During the design process, we decided the facade of the building should be preserved to integrate with the architectural style of the historic neighborhood. However, this proved to be extremely difficult because the existing plan and floor heights had been designed to accommodate apartments, not a space for art. We found it necessary to undertake a significant renovation to demolish and rebuild the interior while maintaining the exterior structure of the building.

After much contemplation regarding the plan, we decided on a simple double-layer configuration of a concrete box gallery embedded in a brick shell. The interstitial space between the concrete and brick walls connects the three layers of the building and becomes a circulation zone. Here, the past and the present can interface amongst the natural light diffusing through the north windows of the historic brick building. We believe the spirit of this architecture prompts a dialogue between the traditional and the contemporary. On the top floor, we added an extension of a new penthouse with a unique skylight. Beneath the northern eaves, a smooth and polished terrace reflects the surrounding tree canopy like a water basin.

The client is incredibly devoted to this neighborhood and considers this area to be his permanent home. He hoped this renovation would add a century to the lifespan of the building, so we scrutinized all details pertaining to durability and maintenance. Through the revitalization of this building, I hope that client's desires were fulfilled and that this architecture becomes an integral part of the neighborhood.

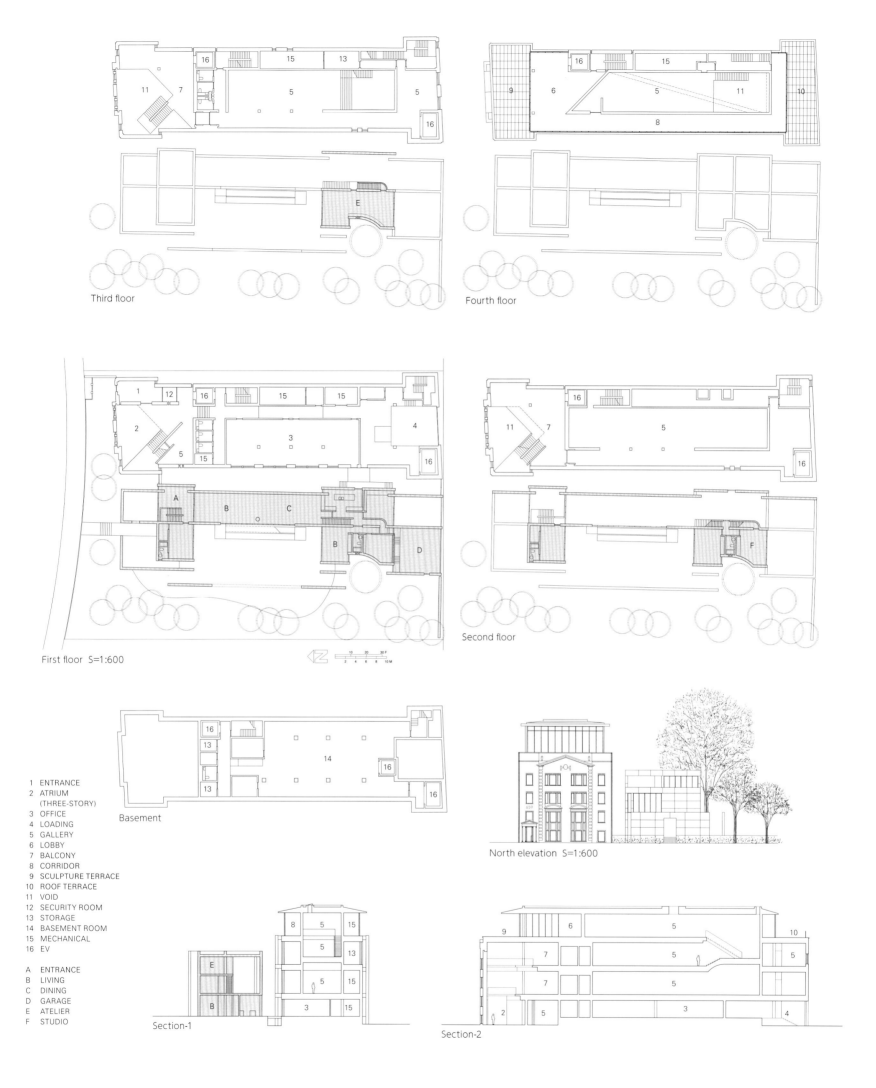

Third floor

Fourth floor

First floor S=1:600

Second floor

Basement

North elevation S=1:600

Section-1

Section-2

1 ENTRANCE
2 ATRIUM
  (THREE-STORY)
3 OFFICE
4 LOADING
5 GALLERY
6 LOBBY
7 BALCONY
8 CORRIDOR
9 SCULPTURE TERRACE
10 ROOF TERRACE
11 VOID
12 SECURITY ROOM
13 STORAGE
14 BASEMENT ROOM
15 MECHANICAL
16 EV

A ENTRANCE
B LIVING
C DINING
D GARAGE
E ATELIER
F STUDIO

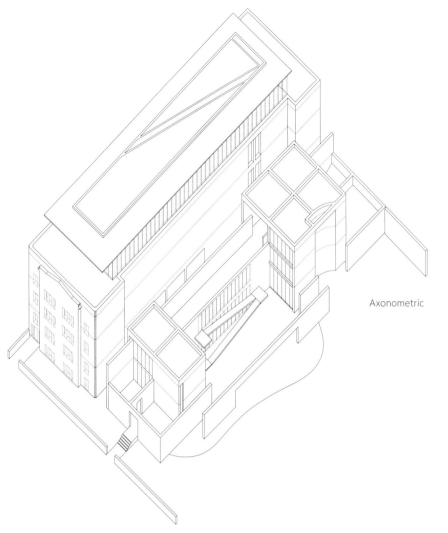

Axonometric

Gap between *House in Chicago* and *Wrightwood 659*
「シカゴの住宅」と「シカゴのギャラリー」の間

View toward entrance　入口を見る

1997年, シカゴの都心に近い, 閑静な住宅地に「シカゴの住宅」を完成させた。我々がアメリカで手掛けた初めての仕事だったが, そのクライアントから, 新たな仕事の依頼を受けた。それが「シカゴの住宅」の隣地に建つ, 90年前に建てられたレンガ造の建築をギャラリーとして改造する, 今回のプロジェクトである。

　街並み保存が計画の前提条件であったが, 既存建物は集合住宅として設計されたものであり, プラン, 階高ともに, そのままではギャラリーへの転用は難しかった。そこで, 建物の外壁, ファサードはそのまま残しつつ, 内部の構造体を完全につくり直すという, 大がかりな改造を行った。

　検討の末に行き着いたのは, レンガ造の外皮の内側をそっくり切り取った後に, ギャラリーを内包するコンクリートのボックスを挿入するという, シンプルな二重構造である。中間領域となる, コンクリートとレンガの狭間の三層吹抜けの空間は, 各階をつなぐサーキュレーション・ゾーンとなる。時間の刻まれたレンガ壁の窓から差し込む自然光のもとに, 過去と現在が対峙する。そこに喚起される新旧の対話が, この建築の精神を象徴する。建物最上部には, 特徴的なトップライトを持つペントハウスを新たに加えた。その北側の庇の下のテラスは, 水盤のように周囲の歴史的風景を映し込む磨石仕上げとなっている。

　この土地を終の棲家として, 街並みに深い愛情を持つクライアントは, 今回の改造によってさらに100年の寿命が建物に与えられることを期待されており, 耐久性, メンテナンス性については慎重に議論を重ねた。今回の計画により新たな息吹を吹き込まれる建物がクライアントの思いに応えて, しっかりと街に息づいていけばと思う。

View toward gallery from landing stairs　踊り場よりギャラリー方向を見る

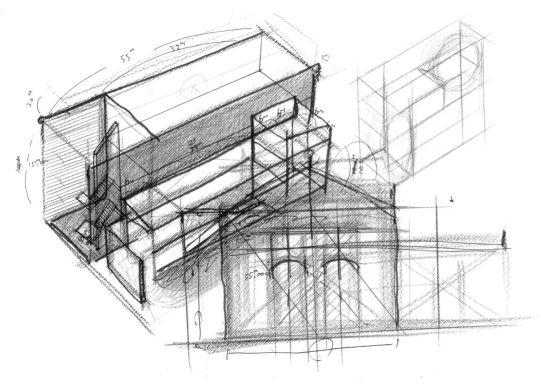

View of atrium from balcony on second floor ▷
2階バルコニーよりアトリウムを見る

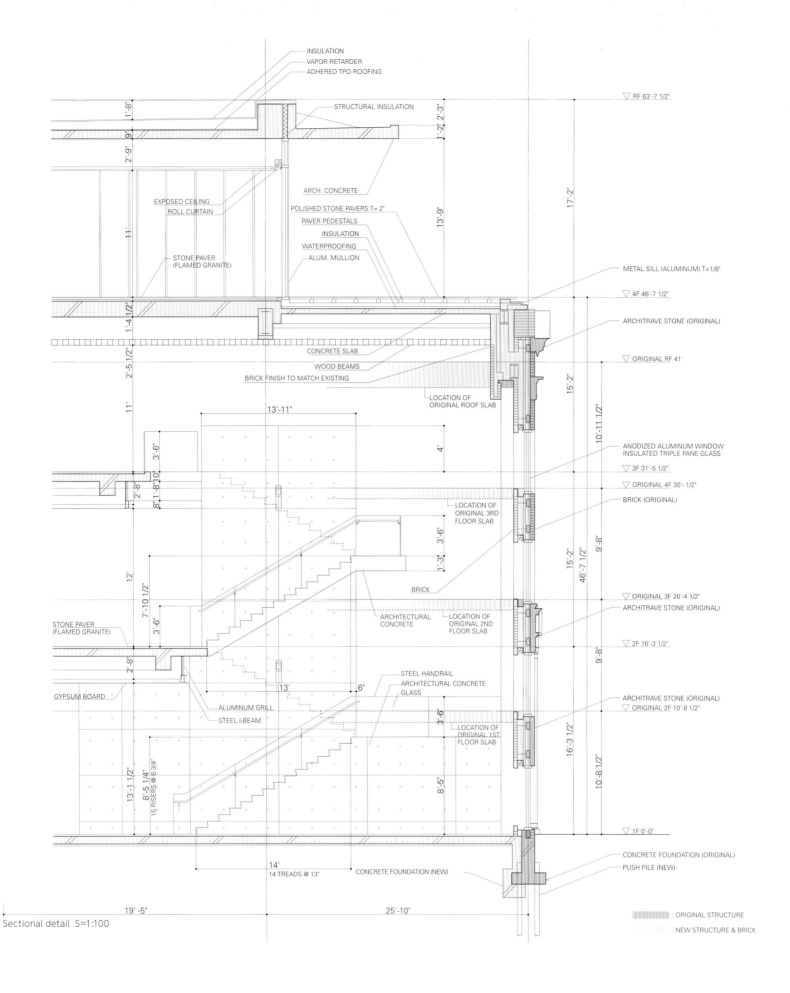

INSULATION
VAPOR RETARDER
ADHERED TPO ROOFING
STRUCTURAL INSULATION

ARCH. CONCRETE
POLISHED STONE PAVERS T= 2"
PAVER PEDESTALS
INSULATION
WATERPROOFING
ALUM. MULLION

EXPOSED CEILING
ROLL CURTAIN

STONE PAVER
(FLAMED GRANITE)

CONCRETE SLAB
WOOD BEAMS
BRICK FINISH TO MATCH EXISTING

LOCATION OF
ORIGINAL ROOF SLAB

LOCATION OF
ORIGINAL 3RD
FLOOR SLAB

BRICK

STONE PAVER
(FLAMED GRANITE)

ARCHITECTURAL
CONCRETE

LOCATION OF
ORIGINAL 2ND
FLOOR SLAB

STEEL HANDRAIL
ARCHITECTURAL CONCRETE
GLASS

GYPSUM BOARD

ALUMINUM GRILL
STEEL I-BEAM

LOCATION OF
ORIGINAL 1ST
FLOOR SLAB

CONCRETE FOUNDATION (NEW)

RF 63'-7 1/2"

METAL SILL (ALUMINUM) T=1/8"

4F 46'-7 1/2"

ARCHITRAVE STONE (ORIGINAL)

ORIGINAL RF 41'

ANODIZED ALUMINUM WINDOW
INSULATED TRIPLE PANE GLASS

3F 31'-5 1/2"
ORIGINAL 4F 30'- 1/2"

BRICK (ORIGINAL)

ORIGINAL 3F 20'-4 1/2"
ARCHITRAVE STONE (ORIGINAL)

2F 16'-3 1/2"

ARCHITRAVE STONE (ORIGINAL)
ORIGINAL 2F 10'-8 1/2"

1F 0'-0"

CONCRETE FOUNDATION (ORIGINAL)
PUSH PILE (NEW)

: ORIGINAL STRUCTURE
: NEW STRUCTURE & BRICK

Sectional detail S=1:100

Brick wall of atrium. Brick is reclaimed from existing building
アトリウムの煉瓦壁。煉瓦は既存建物のものを再利用した

△▽ Construction of brick wall
煉瓦壁の施工

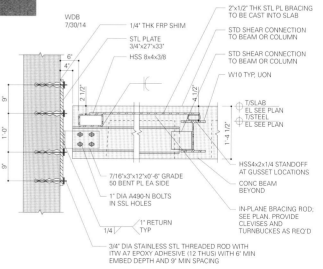

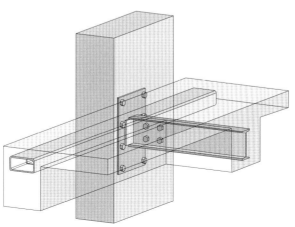

Detail: joint of existing brick wall and steel structure S=1:30

WDB
7/30/14

1/4" THK FRP SHIM

STL PLATE
3/4"x27"x33"

HSS 8x4x3/8

6"

4"

2 1/2"

9"

1'-0"

9"

7/16"x3"x12"x0'-6" GRADE
50 BENT PL EA SIDE

1" DIA A490-N BOLTS
IN SSL HOLES

1/4

1" RETURN
TYP

3/4" DIA STAINLESS STL THREADED ROD WITH
ITW A7 EPOXY ADHESIVE (12 THUS) WITH 6" MIN
EMBED DEPTH AND 9" MIN SPACING

2"x1/2" THK STL PL BRACING
TO BE CAST INTO SLAB

STD SHEAR CONNECTION
TO BEAM OR COLUMN

STD SHEAR CONNECTION
TO BEAM OR COLUMN

W10 TYP, UON

4 1/2"

T/SLAB
EL SEE PLAN
T/STEEL
EL SEE PLAN

1'-4 1/2"

HSS4x2x1/4 STANDOFF
AT GUSSET LOCATIONS

CONC BEAM
BEYOND

IN-PLANE BRACING ROD;
SEE PLAN. PROVIDE
CLEVISES AND
TURNBUCKES AS REQ'D

TYPICAL FACTORED FORCES AT THIS CONNECTION:
Vu = 45 kips
Pu = 5 kips (PARALLEL TO MAJOR AXIS OF MEMBER)

Landing stairs: slit-like opening　踊り場：スリット状の開口

Balcony on second floor: atrium inmost　2階バルコニー：奥にアトリウム

Atrium on first floor: gallery on left　1階アトリウム。左にギャラリー▽

◁ Atrium on first floor　1階アトリウム

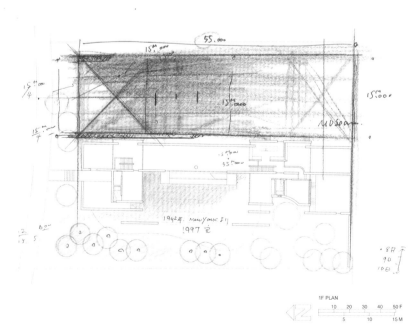

1F PLAN

Balcony on third floor　3階バルコニー

Downward view of stairs from balcony on third floor
3階バルコニーより階段を見下ろす

Galley on third floor　3階ギャラリー

Galley on third floor: balcony inmost　3階ギャラリー。奥にバルコニー

View of gallery with skylight on fourth floor　トップライトのある4階ギャラリーを見る

Lobby on fourth floor: sculpture terrace on left. Stone polished and reflects surrounding
4階ロビー：左にスカルプチャー・テラス。本磨仕上げの石が周辺を映し込む

Corridor on fourth floor　4階回廊

View from southwest over *House in Chicago*
南西より「シカゴの住宅」越しに見る

Taizo Kuroda Gallery
黒田泰蔵ギャラリー

Ito, Shizuoka
静岡県伊東市
2018–20

黒田泰蔵ギャラリー

View from west　西より見る

View of gallery building from southeast　南東よりギャラリー棟を見る

Bird's eye view from west. Existing atelier on right. Site is located on hill overlooking Pacific Ocean　西側上空より見る。右は既存のアトリエ。太平洋を望む丘に位置する

In the October of 2016, I received a call from Taizo Kuroda (a ceramic artist and a friend for over 40 years) requesting a design of a museum to exhibit his works. When asked for the scale, he said the project was around 15 m² and I initially pondered at its "difficulty." This "small-ness," in reconsidering however, had a profound potential to be the appeal of the project and was a challenge I wanted to take.

The site faces the Pacific Ocean, located on a small hill in Izu Island's east-ern edge with a vista of Sagami bay. Kuroda held his atelier there, surrounded by nature and woods. It is in this forest where we made a modest gallery.

Serene and refined, Taizo Kuroda's delicate form of porcelain pottery is renowned globally. Thus, the aim was to reside this power of silence within the exhibition space to complement Kuro-da's work.

The building was completed in the August of 2020. Although Taizo Kuroda regrettably passed away in the April of 2021, the gallery, created through the crashing of our ideas, will leave Kuroda's enduring thoughts to future generations.

Site plan with sketch S=1:800

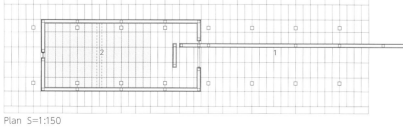

Plan S=1:150

South elevation S=1:150

View toward pilotis from south　南よりピロティを見る

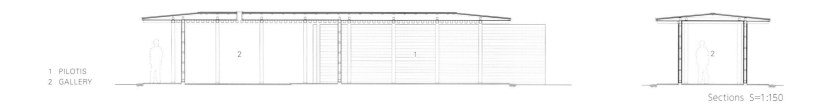

1　PILOTIS
2　GALLERY

Sections　S=1:150

View toward entrance through pilotis from east　東よりピロティ越しに入口を見る

Entrance 入口

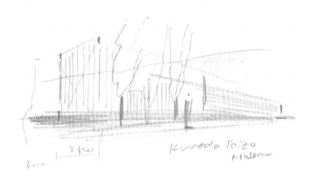

Tadao Ando

Detail of eaves edge　軒先のディテール

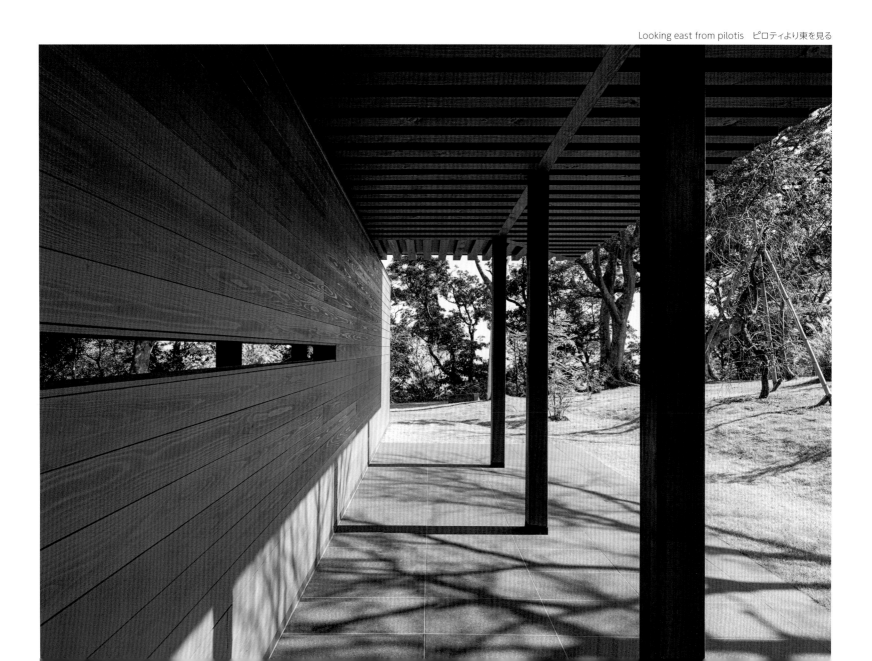

Corner on southwest　南西角部

2016年の10月, 黒田泰蔵さんから電話があり, 作品を展示する美術館をつくりたいので設計をお願いしたいとの依頼を受けた。どのくらいの規模のものかと聞くと, 15m²ほどだと言うので, はじめは「難しいな」と思った。しかし, 〈小さい〉ということは一つの魅力になるのではないかと思い直し, 引き受けることにした。

　敷地は伊豆半島の東端, 相模湾を遠望する小高い丘の上に位置する。自然の樹々に囲まれたその場所で, 黒田氏は自身のアトリエを構えていた。その森の一画に, ささやかなギャラリーをつくった。

　既存のアトリエのひっそりとした佇まいにならい, 木の建築とした。必要最小限の構造で支える屋根の下の約半分は, 外部空間となっている。文字通りの〈縁側〉のようなギャラリーだ。ギャラリー内部の採光は, 天井に穿たれた幅10cmのスリットからの光のみ。日の出と共に目覚め, 日没とともに眠りにつく。黒田泰蔵さんのつくる静謐な白磁の造形に相応しい, 静かな力を秘めた空間となることを目指した。

　ギャラリー内部の床には水が張られており, その鏡面上に白磁の作品が浮かぶ。この水の空間のアイディアは, 工事の終盤に現地を訪れた黒田さんより提案を受け, 実現した。建物は2020年の8月に完成した。残念ながら黒田泰蔵さんは, 2021年の4月に亡くなられたが, お互いの思いをぶつけながらつくりあげたギャラリーは, 黒田さんの遺志を後世にしっかりと伝えていくだろう。

4.500　　4.500

Tadao Ando

Gallery. Floor is covered with water and reflect interior
ギャラリー。床には水が張られ, 室内を反射する

Gallery: natural light comes through slit-shaped skylight　ギャラリー：スリット状の天窓より自然光が落ちる

LG Art Center

LGアートセンター

Seoul, South Korea
韓国, ソウル
2015-22

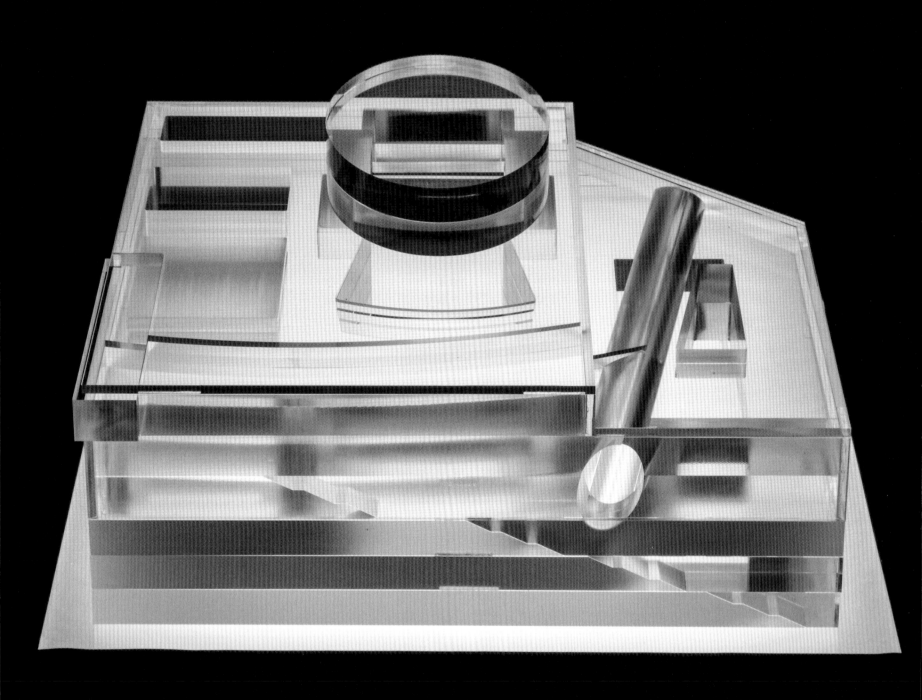

Concept model　コンセプト模型

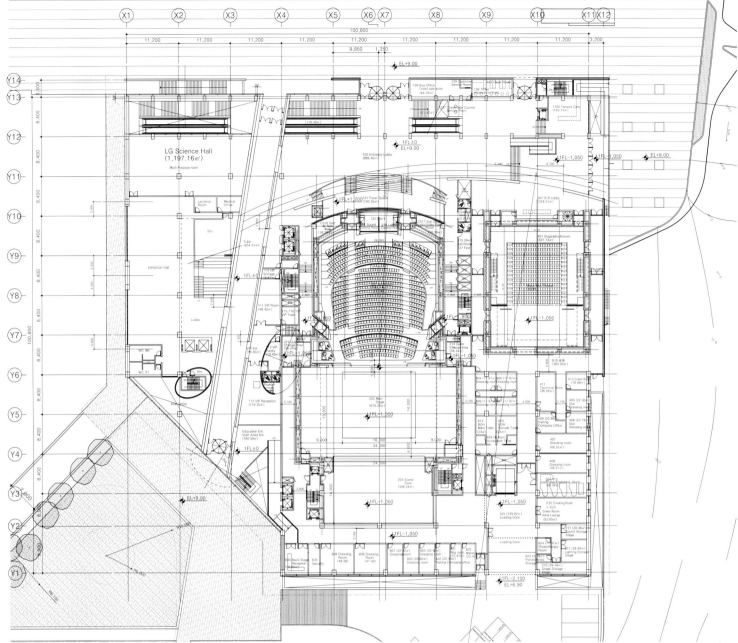

First floor S=1:800

The site is located in Magok Park in Gangseo-gu, at the western edge of Seoul, South Korea, in the proximity of Gimpo Airport. *The LG Art Center* is the core to an ongoing urban development project in the park encompassing: a 1,300-seat multipurpose hall, *Art Center*; and an interactive science museum, *Science Hall*.

The client, LG Group, has been operating the former LG Art Center in Yeoksam-dong, Gangnam-gu, for over 20 years. After consulting with the Seoul Metropolitan Government, the group has obtained a new location for the renewal of the hall.

The architecture was planned based on a square plan lengthening over 100-meter with an overlay of diagonal lines running across the north-south direction. Stretching out from the entrance court in the south is a promenade approach that defines the boundary between the east and the west volume. *The Art Center* on the east is approximately 21 m high with three floors, and *the Science Hall* on the west is approximately 12 m high with two floors. The rooftop of the Science Hall is a roof garden that resonates with the surrounding greenery.

There are mainly three distinctive elements that define the 41,500 m² of interior space in total, ranging from 3 floors below ground to 3 floors above ground: the "Catalyst Tube," which runs through the building between the two zones; The "Step Atrium" covers the northwest edge; and the "Gate Arc," which appears as the facade to the hall. The "Catalyst Tube" is the main element of the building. It is a tube-shaped space with an elliptical cross-section that dynamically connects the north and south sides of the site and spatially interweaves the art and science zone. The "Step Atrium" is the fundamental element for the circulation of the facility. The atrium connects all levels vertically along the plaza on the north side and is an open space at ground level connecting to the park. The "Gate Arc" is a curved concrete wall that encloses the two halls of *the Art Center*, the main hall, and the black box. It forms a gate that serves as the entrance of each.

The facility will be donated to the city of Seoul after its completion and will be operated by the LG Group for the next 20 years. This project will represent another unique method to establish new public cultural facilities.

Construction site　工事現場

Tube　チューブ

Construction site　工事現場

Entrance lobby　エントランス・ロビー

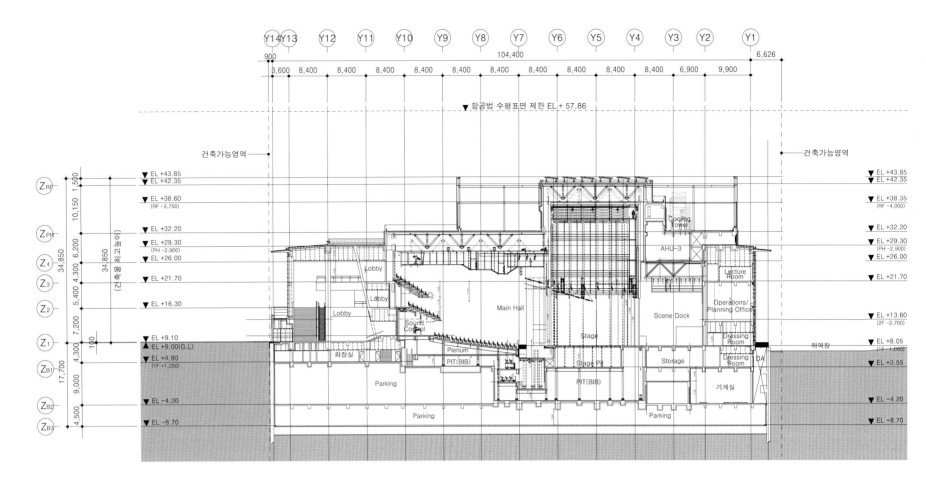

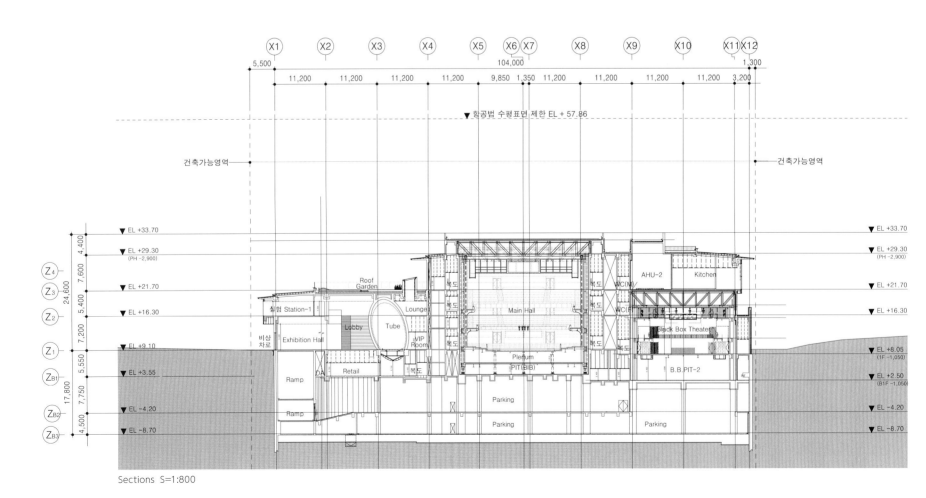

Sections S=1:800

Overall view from north　北より見る全景

敷地は韓国ソウル市西端，金浦空港がある江西区の麻谷公園内に位置する。同公園内で進行中の都市開発プロジェクトの一つの核として計画された，1,300人収容の多目的ホール（アートセンター）と体験型の科学博物館（サイエンスホール）を含む複合文化施設の計画である。

クライアントであるLGグループは，江南区の駅三洞で20年以上にわたりホール（『旧LGアートセンター』）を運営してきた実績がある。その老朽化による建替え計画にあたり，グループはソウル市と協議，新たな立地を得るに至った。

建物は，南北方向に対角線をあわせた100m角の正方形平面を基本として計画されており，南方向の一角が，アプローチコートの用に充てられている。アプローチから向かって東側がアートセンター，西側がサイエンスホールで，前者が三層約21mの高さ，後者が二層約12mと，それぞれに異なるヴォリュームを持つ。「サイエンス」ブロックの屋上は緑を配したルーフガーデンとなり，周囲の公園の緑地と呼応する。

地下3階から地上3階に及ぶ約41,500m²の内部空間を規定するのは，二つのゾーンの狭間で建物を貫く「カタリスト・チューブ」と，正方形北西の一辺を占める「ステップ・アトリウム」，そして施設内におけるホールのファサードを形成する「ゲート・アーク」という三つの特徴的なエレメントである。「カタリスト・チューブ」は，楕円形断面のチューブ状空間で，敷地の南北をダイナミックに接続するのと同時に，「アート」と「サイエンス」，二つのゾーンを空間的に関係づける。「ステップ・アトリウム」は北側のプラザに沿って全層を垂直方向につなぐ施設のサーキュレーションの要であり，地上部の開放的な空間で公園と連続する。「ゲート・アーク」はコンクリートによる曲面壁の造形で，アートセンターのメインホールとブラック・ボックスの二つのホールを内包しつつ，それぞれの〈顔〉となるゲートを形成する。

施設は竣工後，ソウル市に寄付され，以降20年間はLGグループによって運営される。公共文化施設の新しい在り方として興味深い。

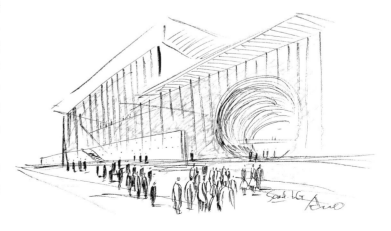

Tadao Ando

Penthouse in Manhattan III
マンハッタンのペントハウス III

New York, U.S.A.
アメリカ合衆国, ニューヨーク州, ニューヨーク
2013-19

Distant view of penthouse with lush green from south
南側遠景。青々とした緑とペントハウスを見る

This is the project for the third penthouse in Manhattan, which follows *the Penthouse in Manhattan* planned in 1996, and *the Penthouse in Manhattan II* completed in the Soho area in New York City in 2008.

The site is the top floor and the rooftop of a 12-storybuilding, which stands on the south-east corner of Lexington Avenue in the Upper East Side. This area has been known as a cultural and exclusive residential place since the beginning of the 20th century. The building was constructed in 1912 and has been designated as a historical landmark which has to be preserved. My client has been running a modern art gallery in NYC for many years and hoped to have a residence in Manhattan. He requested that his residence should be combined with a gallery, and should be something that could be regarded as an artwork. To fulfill the wish, I proposed an ambitious plan for utilizing the rooftop, which might be equal to the uncompleted project of the first Penthouse in 1996.

Functional spaces such as a gallery, living room, dining room and bedrooms are contained on the 12th floor. However, the core of the residence is a penthouse on the rooftop which can be accessed via a winding staircase from the living room. It is a glass-walled "living room in the sky," which provides a great view of skyscrapers and is connected to the roof terrace by a fresh green grass wall, which covers a wall of the rooftop and lies both inside and outside of the penthouse. The fresh green grass wall was implemented with the cooperation of Patrick Blanc, a French artist. Because of the difficulties with the techniques and legal restrictions, but also problems happening at the site, the construction period was greatly extended. However, the passion of my client brought it to completion. What gives drive to an architectural project is the determination of the client, who in this case was certain that "I will live here."

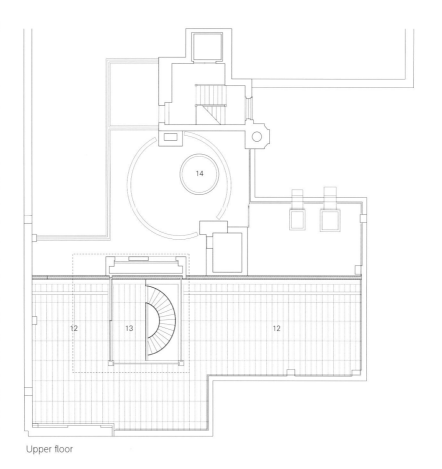

Upper floor

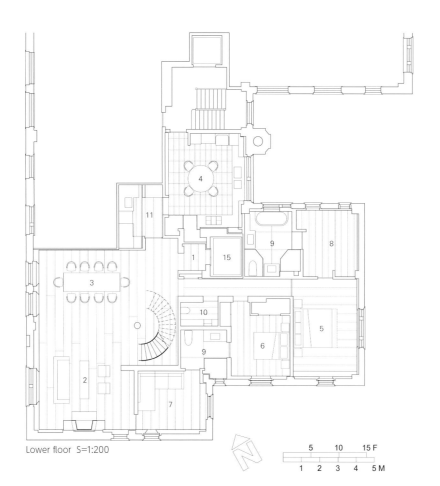

Lower floor S=1:200

1   ENTRANCE
2   LIVING ROOM
3   DINING ROOM
4   KITCHEN
5   MASTER BEDROOM
6   GUEST ROOM
7   STUDY
8   WALK-IN CLOSET
9   BATHROOM
10 POWDER ROOM
11 LAUNDRY
12 TERRACE
13 PENTHOUSE
14 SKYLIGHT
15 ELEVATOR

Concept image (elevation)

1996年に計画した「マンハッタンのペントハウス」，その後2008年にソーホー地区に完成させた「マンハッタンのペントハウスII」に続く，マンハッタンでの，3回目のペントハウスの計画である。

　今回の計画地は20世紀初頭から文化の薫り高い高級住宅地として知られているアッパー・イーストサイド，その南寄り，レキシントン・アベニューの南東角に建つ，12階建てのビルの最上階及び屋上である。ビルは1912年築で，保存義務のある歴史的ランドマークにも指定されていた。長年ニューヨークで，現代美術の画廊を営み，マンハッタンに住まいを構えることを夢としていたクライアントは，ここに空間そのものがアートと呼べるような，ギャラリー兼住宅をつくることを期待していた。それに応えるべく，未完に終わった1996年のプロポーザルに匹敵するような，大胆な屋上階の利用を考えた。

　ギャラリーにリビング，ダイニング，ベッドルーム。必要な機能は全て主階である12階に収まっている。しかし，本当の意味でのこの住居の核心は，リビングから，螺旋状の階段でアプローチする，屋上のペントハウスだ。ガラス張りの空間は，内外を貫いて建物全幅に伸びる緑の壁に沿って東西のルーフ・テラスと連続し，摩天楼の風景を一望におさめる，文字通りの〈空の居間〉だ。緑の壁は，フランスのアーティスト，パトリック・ブランの協力を得て実現された。法規的・技術的に難しいところもあり，更に現場のトラブルも重なって工期は大幅に延びたが，クライアントの執念で，完成に漕ぎつけた。建築に意志を吹き込むのは，やはり，「ここに棲むのだ」というクライアントの意志の力である。

View toward penthouse from terrace　テラスよりペントハウスを見る

View toward fresh green grass wall cooperated with Patrick Blanc from penthouse
ペントハウスより, パトリック・ブラン協力のもとつくられた緑の壁を見る

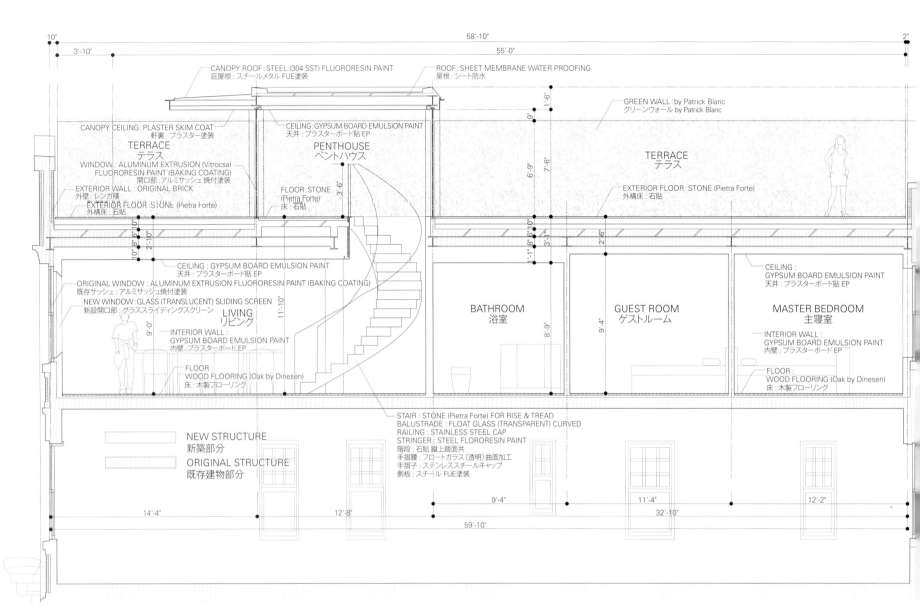

10"   58'-10"   2"

3'-10"   55'-0"

CANOPY ROOF : STEEL (304 SST) FLUORORESIN PAINT
庇屋根：スチールメタル FUE塗装

ROOF : SHEET MEMBRANE WATER PROOFING
屋根：シート防水

CANOPY CEILING : PLASTER SKIM COAT
軒裏：プラスター塗装

CEILING : GYPSUM BOARD EMULSION PAINT
天井：プラスターボード貼 EP

GREEN WALL : by Patrick Blanc
グリーンウォール by Patrick Blanc

TERRACE
テラス

PENTHOUSE
ペントハウス

TERRACE
テラス

WINDOW : ALUMINUM EXTRUSION (Vitrocsa)
FLUORORESIN PAINT (BAKING COATING)
開口部：アルミサッシュ 焼付塗装

EXTERIOR WALL : ORIGINAL BRICK
外壁：レンガ積

FLOOR : STONE
(Pietra Forte)
床：石貼

EXTERIOR FLOOR : STONE (Pietra Forte)
外構床：石貼

EXTERIOR FLOOR : STONE (Pietra Forte)
外構床：石貼

CEILING : GYPSUM BOARD EMULSION PAINT
天井：プラスターボード貼 EP

CEILING :
GYPSUM BOARD EMULSION PAINT
天井：プラスターボード貼 EP

ORIGINAL WINDOW : ALUMINUM EXTRUSION FLUORORESIN PAINT (BAKING COATING)
既存サッシュ：アルミサッシュ焼付塗装

NEW WINDOW : GLASS (TRANSLUCENT) SLIDING SCREEN
新設開口部：グラススライディングスクリーン

LIVING
リビング

BATHROOM
浴室

GUEST ROOM
ゲストルーム

MASTER BEDROOM
主寝室

INTERIOR WALL :
GYPSUM BOARD EMULSION PAINT
内壁：プラスターボード EP

INTERIOR WALL :
GYPSUM BOARD EMULSION PAINT
内壁：プラスターボード EP

FLOOR :
WOOD FLOORING (Oak by Dinesen)
床：木製フローリング

FLOOR :
WOOD FLOORING (Oak by Dinesen)
床：木製フローリング

STAIR : STONE (Pietra Forte) FOR RISE & TREAD
BALUSTRADE : FLOAT GLASS (TRANSPARENT) CURVED
RAILING : STAINLESS STEEL CAP
STRINGER : STEEL FLORORESIN PAINT
階段：石貼 蹴上踏面共
手摺腰：フロートガラス（透明）曲面加工
手摺子：ステンレススチールキャップ
側板：スチール FUE塗装

NEW STRUCTURE
新築部分

ORIGINAL STRUCTURE
既存建物部分

14'-4"   12'-8"   9'-4"   11'-4"   12'-2"

32'-10"

59'-10"

Sectional detail S=1:80

EL
204'-2"
2'-3"
9'-0"
6'-9"

EL
192'-4"
11'-10"
11'-0"

EL
181'-2"
11'-2"

View toward terrace on east from penthouse　ペントハウスより東側のテラスを見る

Tadao Ando

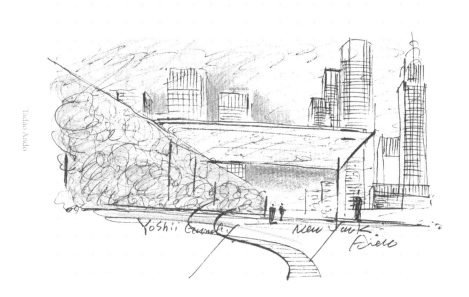

Dining room on lower floor. Spiral stair leads to penthouse　下階, ダイニング・ルーム。螺旋階段はペントハウスに通じる

Living room on lower floor　下階, リビング・ルーム

He Art Museum
和美術館
Foshan, Guangdong, China
中国広東省仏山市
2014-20

Overall view from northwest　北西より見る全景

This museum is located in an industrial development area in the city of Foshan in Guangdong Province, China. My client is a member of a family that founded a global company originating in the city of Foshan. The project started based on the desire of my client to make a cultural contribution to his home town, and to present his collections of traditional arts and modern art to the public.

The area around the site is highly urbanized. To the north and the east, the museum is adjacent to the headquarters' buildings of the affiliated companies he owns, and to the south, there is a public park. We aimed at creating harmony and peace through art and culture, and the project was named *He Art Museum*, since the Chinese character "he" has the

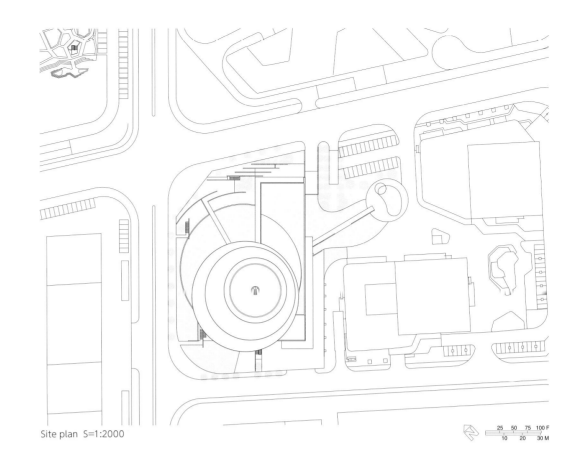

Site plan S=1:2000

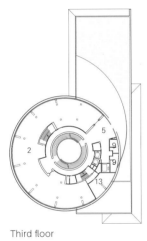

Third floor

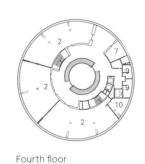

Fourth floor

Fifth floor

Roof

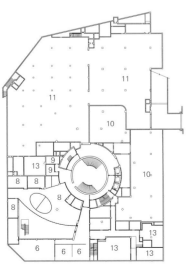

Basement floor S=1:1600

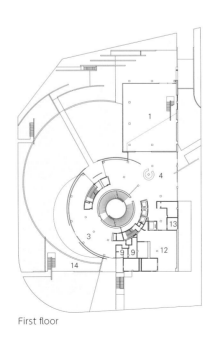

First floor

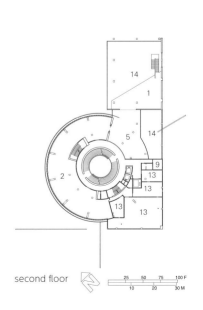

second floor

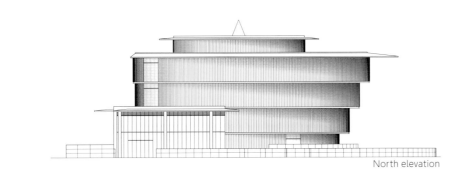

North elevation

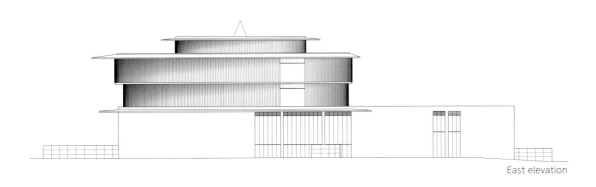

East elevation

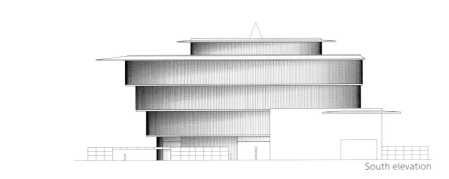

South elevation

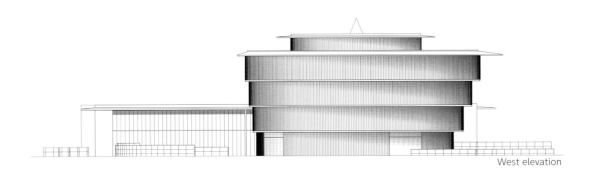

West elevation

1 SPECIAL EXHIBITION HALL
2 GALLERY
3 CAFE
4 ENTRANCE
5 LOUNGE
6 CLASSROOM
7 VIP ROOM
8 OFFICE
9 RESTROOM
10 STORAGE
11 PARKING
12 LOADING
13 MECHANICAL
14 VOID

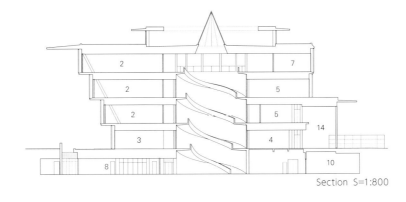

Section S=1:800

meaning of harmony. Meanwhile, the Lingnan culture, which has been cultivated in the region, has an essence of strength based on continental Chinese culture, and it uses the shape of the circle in its designs, from craftworks to architecture, as a motif for traditional Chinese philosophies. As an urban museum, it had to achieve a good balance between contrasting concepts, i.e. between tranquility and activeness, and between the gathering and presentation of cultural elements, while always retaining the spirit of the Lingnan culture. As a consequence, we decided to try to create architecture including the motif of the circle shape.

The buildings have two simple divisions; the main one is round and the other is square. The circles in the space of the round building expand, overlapping and misaligning their centers, with varying scales and heights. Overall, this represents an image which gently expands from the inside to the outside, from the architecture of the buildings to the town. The middle of the overlapping circles is a space centering on a double-helix staircase with an open ceiling to the fifth floor. The round building has authentic and practical functions such as exhibition rooms for traditional art pieces and public educational facilities. On the other hand, the square building provides a space for modern art activities including cultural events and performing arts. The spatial overlap, which is made by symbolic, simple geometries, create architectural scenes and a sense of rhythm, which has become the primary characteristic of the He Art Museum.

In addition, for the vacant space in the site, I designed a landscape under the theme of water, as a park where citizens can come and enjoy their time. The water garden is set there matching the round shape of the museum building, and it can work as a cooling device during the severe summer of the sub-tropical climate. The surface of the water reflects the architecture and the water garden appears to form the base of the building.

Evening view of water basin　水盤夕景

Approach to entrance　エントランスへのアプローチ

中国広東省仏山市，振興開発エリアにたつ美術館である。クライアントは，同市を発祥の地とする世界的企業の創業家。故郷への文化貢献の一環として，蒐集してきた伝統芸術，現代アートのコレクションを公開したいという彼の思いからプロジェクトは始まった。

　敷地は，北側，東側にクライアントの所有する関連企業の本社ビル，南に市民公園に近接する極めて都市性の高い場所に位置する。芸術，文化による調和，平和を主題として，プロジェクトは「和美術館」と名付けられていた。一方で，この地域で育まれてきた嶺南文化は，とりわけ大陸ならではの強さを感じさせる文化であり，〈陰陽調和〉，〈合祥協和〉を象徴する形として，建築から工芸に至るまで，〈円〉が様々な形で用いられていた。静寂さと活発さ，求心力と発信力。都市の美術館に求められる，これらの対立的な特性を，嶺南文化の精神のもとに両立させるべく，我々は，円形をモチーフとする建築を試みた。

　建物は，単純な円形と方形による建築構成を持つ。中心となる円形棟の空間は，重心とスケール，高さを変えながらズレ重なり，内から外へ，建築から都市へと緩やかに広がるイメージで展開する。積層する〈円〉の中核を成すのは，二重らせん階段のめぐる五層吹抜けの空間である。この力強い垂直の空間が，各階を視覚的につなぐのと同時に，〈二重〉ならではの多様なサーキュレーションを可能にする。円形棟には伝統芸術の展示や，公共教育施設など，ヒューマンスケールな機能がおさめられる。対して，大空間を持つ方形棟は，文化イベントやパフォーマンス芸術など，現代的で多様な活動の受け皿となる。これらの象徴的な単純幾何学の立体的交錯がつくり出す陰影深い建築の風景，そこに醸し出される場所の躍動感が，唯一無二の「和美術館」の個性である。

　敷地内の余白は，人々が憩える公園として，水を主題とするランドスケープを計画した。〈円〉と呼応するように広がる水盤は，亜熱帯の厳しい夏季の気候を和らげる親水装置であり，同時に，その表面に建築を映し出し，個性を引き立てる〈台座〉である。

View from north. Fours volumes stacking and shifting their gravitational centers.
北より見る。重心をずらしながら四つのヴォリュームが重なる

△▽ Gallery on second floor　2階展示室

Gallery on third floor　3階展示室

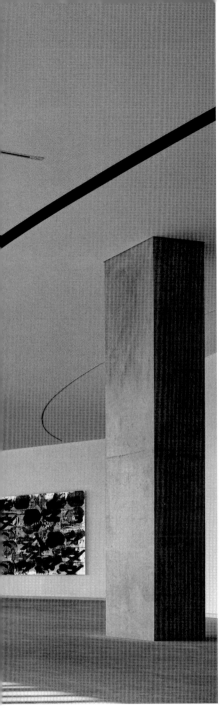

Special exhibition hall on first floor of square building　方形棟1階特別展示ホール

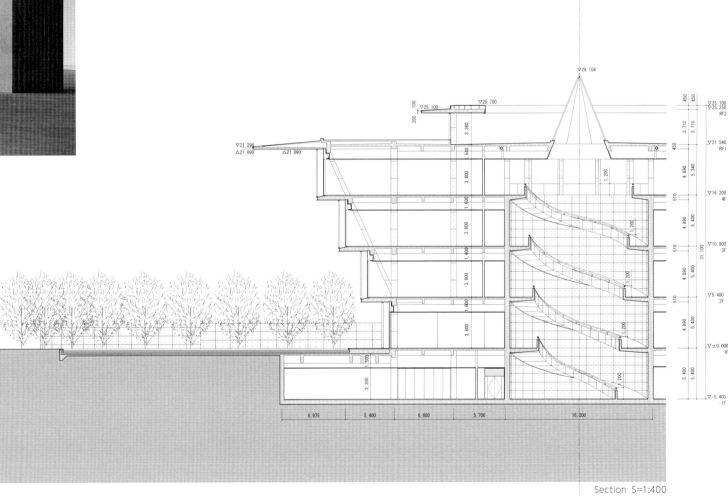

Section　S=1:400

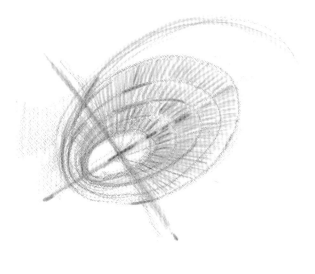

◁ Downward view of double spiral staircase in atrium
アトリウムの二重螺旋階段を見下ろす

Upward view of atrium　アトリウムの見上げ

Atrium on basement floor　地下1階アトリウム

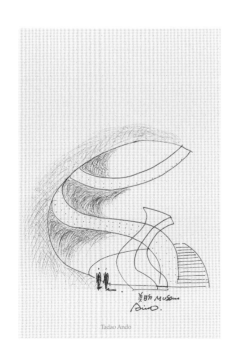

Tadao Ando

Atrium. Natural light through light-well ▷
アトリウム。天窓より差し込む自然光

IPU (International Pacific University) "Discovery", "Harmony", "Inspire"

IPU・環太平洋大学 ［Discovery］，［Harmony］，［Inspire］

Okayama, Okayama

岡山県岡山市
2014-19, 2015-16, 2017-18

Aerial view from south　南側上空より見る

The site is located in the suburbs of Okayama City, Okayama Prefecture, in a foothill area surrounded by rich greenery. *The DISCOVERY* is a new educational facility in the IPU–International Pacific University campus which was established in 2007.

I became acquainted with Ohashi Sensei (Mr. Hiroshi Ohashi, the Chair of the Board of Trustees, IPU/Soshi Gakuen) in the early 2000s. Ohashi Sensei began his educational career at a small tutoring school in Kobe. In a period of a few decades, he established the Soshi Educational Group which encompasses kindergartens, high schools, vocational colleges, universities, and institutes of higher education. Even before we began to collaborate, I had heard of his outstanding business prowess. Upon our first meeting, I was astounded by his absolute trust in the power of education to empower the world as well as his passion for creating excellent progressive school facilities which strayed from existing institutional frameworks. One of the challenging goals which Ohashi Sensei set for himself in education was to establish an entirely new university. The unique concept of this facility was to integrate academic and physical education.

My first commission was to design the martial art athlete hall, *TOPGUN*, which is

placed on the central axis of the campus. Ohashi Sensei's words were, "Buildings should be more than just functional. I want them to be environments which nurture human capabilities." With these words as my compass, I designed a site-specific structure that became a symbolic "gate," which connects the campus and its students to the future. I incorporated stairs into the entirety of the roof to produce a fully functional open space.

The design was intended to create an environment that makes the whole building a place for physical training.

It was during the construction of *TOPGUN* when I was asked to begin the next project, an instructional facility known as *PHILOSOPHIA*. This was followed by a series of projects: *HARMONY*, the cafeteria; INSPIRE, the sports science center; and *DISCOVERY*, the newest instructional facility which was recently completed in 2019.

After designing one project after another over the span of ten years or so, I have now completed five buildings on the campus.

Designing a university campus would normally begin with a master plan, followed by a scheduled and coordinated process of construction, but Ohashi Sensei was not concerned with conventional planning methods. He seemed to take one step forward at a time, carefully thinking about the sites and buildings and

Aerial view from north. *Topgun* in center, *Discovery* on left above, *Harmony* on left below　北側より見る。真ん中に［Topgun］，左上に［Discovery］，左下に［Harmony］

speaking with the lecturers and students who would eventually use these spaces to teach and learn. I also valued the nature of this dialogue and would reflect upon it whenever I embarked on a new project for the campus.

Each of the buildings is distinct and independent, with its own programs and spaces, yet shares commonalities in design elements such as expansive *Engawa* (veranda) spaces with large eaves supported by colonnades, long stone walls running parallel to approach sequences, and the front courtyards playing hide-and-seek between them. These elements serve to frame views of the campus and visually unite the old and new university buildings. The campus structures are akin to a unique assortment of trees in an ancient forest, each varying in attributes yet contributing equally to a delicate equilibrium.

Ohashi Sensei is quite fond of the concept of the "Forest of Learning" found at this campus.

敷地は，岡山県岡山市郊外の緑豊かな丘陵地に位置する。2007年に同地に開学したIPU・環太平洋大学の新校舎の計画である。

クライアントである，大橋先生（大橋博理事長）とは2000年に知り合った。幼稚園から，高校，専門学校，大学までを手掛ける，創志学園グループを一代で築き上げたすぐれた経営者だ。直に対面して強く感じたのは，「教育こそが世界の力の源である」という〈教育〉に対する絶対の信頼と，「だからこそ，教育の現場は，既成の枠組みに捉われない，自由で柔軟な発想で創らねばならない」という教育環境づくりへの情熱だった。そんな大橋先生の〈教育〉における挑戦の集大成が，教育と体育の融合をコンセプトとするこの大学である。

最初に依頼を受けたのは，キャンパスの中心軸上に建つ武道館[TOPGUN]の設計だった。「機能のための施設ではない，人間を育てる環境をつくってほしい」という大橋先生の言葉を頼りに，立地に相応しく，キャンパスとそこで学ぶ学生たちの新たな未来へとつながるゲートを象徴するような形で，さらに屋根面の全てが階段広場となるよう計画した。建物そのものがトレーニングの場となるような環境づくりを意図した設計だった。

次なるプロジェクトとして学舎[PHILO-SOPHIA]の設計依頼を受けたのは，武道館がいまだ工事中の時である。その後も，プロジェクトは続き，カフェテリア[HARMONY]，スポーツ科学センター[INSPIRE]と段階的に建設を重ね，そして2019年に五つ目となる新学舎[DISCOVERY]が完成した。

キャンパス計画というと，マスタープランを定め，予定調和的につくっていく形が普通だろう。だが大橋先生は，そうした従来型の計画手法に囚われることなく，つくりながら，関係する場所と建物，先生や学生たちとの対話を重ねながら，一歩一歩前に進んでおられるように見える。キャンパス計画で新たなプロジェクトに取り組む度，私が大切に考えたのもまた，この対話の精神だった。既存の校舎を含めた建物一つひとつが，それぞれに自立しながら，列柱の支える大庇の〈縁側〉テラス，アプローチを形づくる石の壁，その背後に見え隠れする前庭などを介して視覚的，空間的につながり，響き合う。個性的な木々が集まって一つの森を形づくるイメージだ。

その「学びの森」の新たな核となるべく構想された[DISCOVERY]は，企業人，教育者育成に向けた実践型能力トレーニングのための施設である。学生のプレゼン力・企画提案力を育むための重要なフィールドとしての役割を果たす。このプログラムに応えるべく，[PHILO-SOPHIA]以来の〈縁側〉のコンセプトの集大成のような建築を目指した。交差する新旧のキャンパス軸により導かれた大屋根の下，矩形と楕円のヴォリュームが並び，その間に，自然の光と風を持つ余白の空間——そこで多様な対話，交流の場が展開する。アプローチの前庭としてつくられた水盤が，その情景を静かに映し出す。

大橋先生は，[DISCOVERY]までを，キャンパスづくりの第一段階だと言う。続く第二段階にはいかなる世界が広がるのか。〈学びの森〉の成長は続いていく。

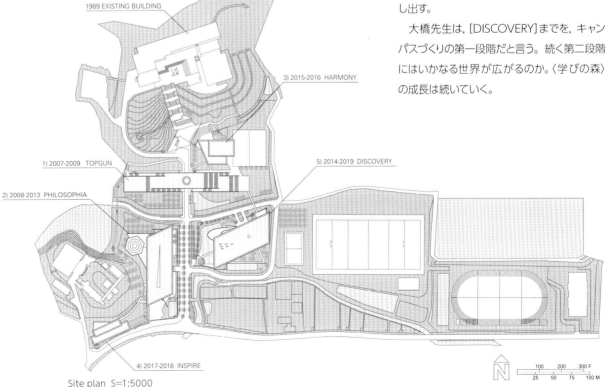

1989 EXISTING BUILDING

3) 2015-2016 HARMONY

1) 2007-2009 TOPGUN

5) 2014-2019 DISCOVERY

2) 2008-2013 PHILOSOPHIA

4) 2017-2018 INSPIRE

Site plan S=1:5000

100   200   300 F

25   50   75   100 M

"Discovery"

△View across water court from west　西より水盤越しに見る

▽ View from northwest　北西より見る

View from under eaves. Slope to second floor
軒下より見る。2階に続くスロープ

View from northwest. Learning lab on left
北西より見下ろす。左にラーニングラボ

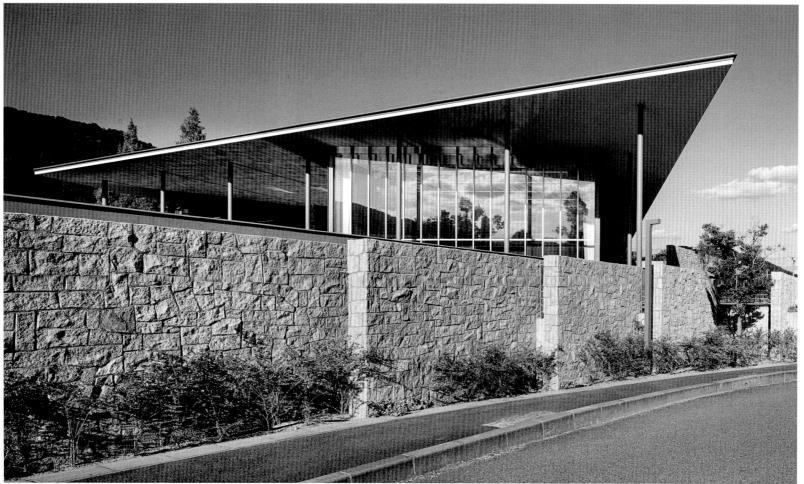

View from west　西より見る

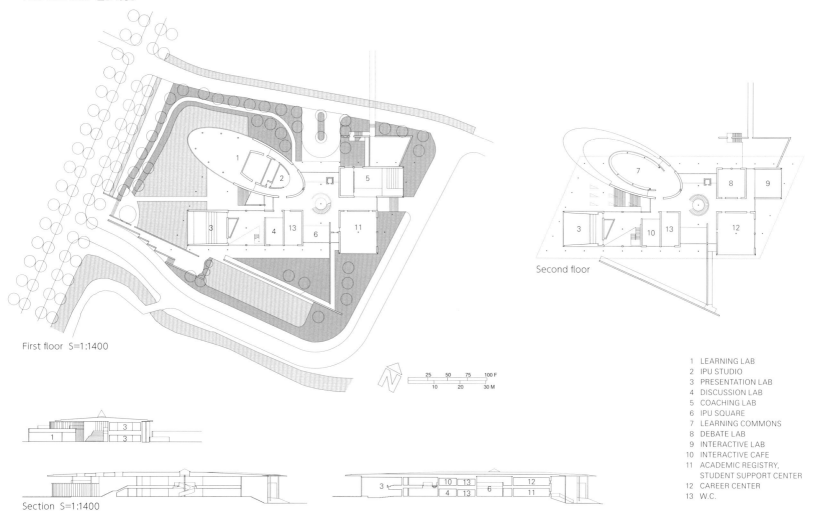

First floor　S=1:1400

Second floor

Section　S=1:1400

1　LEARNING LAB
2　IPU STUDIO
3　PRESENTATION LAB
4　DISCUSSION LAB
5　COACHING LAB
6　IPU SQUARE
7　LEARNING COMMONS
8　DEBATE LAB
9　INTERACTIVE LAB
10　INTERACTIVE CAFE
11　ACADEMIC REGISTRY,
　　STUDENT SUPPORT CENTER
12　CAREER CENTER
13　W.C.

Evening view from northwest　北西より見る夕景

View from grand stairs. *PHILOSOPHIA* inmost
大階段より西を見る。奥に［PHILOSOPHIA］

Looking learning lab　ラーニングラボを見る

Downward view of approach　アプローチを見下ろす△

▽View of entrance with skylight from southwest　南西よりトップライトのある入口を見る

Downward view of spiral staircase　螺旋階段を見下ろす

Spiral staircase　螺旋階段

Presentation lab　プレゼンテーションラボ

Learning lab on first floor　1階ラーニングラボ

Void facing on discussion lab　ディスカッションラボに面する吹抜け

"Harmony"

View from northwest. *TOPGUN* on right　北西より見る。右に[TOPGUN]

Bridge to terrace on second floor　2階テラスにつながるブリッジ

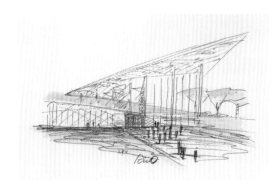

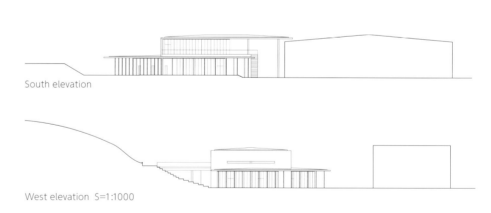

South elevation

West elevation S=1:1000

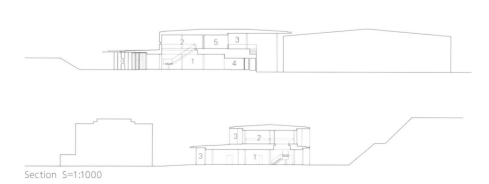

Section S=1:1000

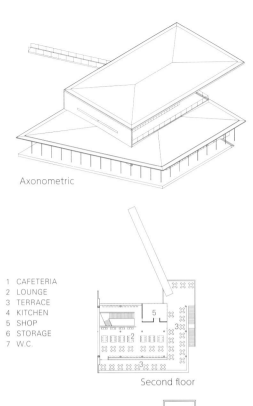

Axonometric

1 CAFETERIA
2 LOUNGE
3 TERRACE
4 KITCHEN
5 SHOP
6 STORAGE
7 W.C.

Second floor

First floor S=1:1000

PLAN
10 20 30 40 50 F
5 10   15 M

Terrace under eaves　軒下のテラス

View from south　南より見る

"Inspire"

Overall view from southeast　南東から見る全景

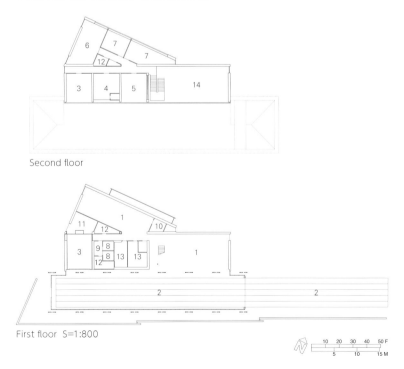

Second floor

First floor S=1:800

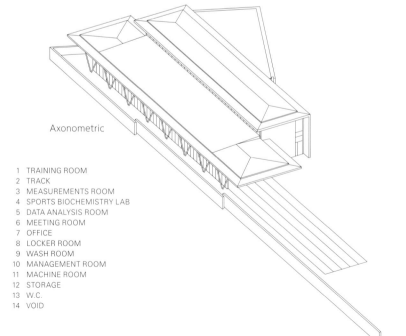

Axonometric

1　TRAINING ROOM
2　TRACK
3　MEASUREMENTS ROOM
4　SPORTS BIOCHEMISTRY LAB
5　DATA ANALYSIS ROOM
6　MEETING ROOM
7　OFFICE
8　LOCKER ROOM
9　WASH ROOM
10　MANAGEMENT ROOM
11　MACHINE ROOM
12　STORAGE
13　W.C.
14　VOID

Track　走路

View toward west under eaves　軒下より西を見る

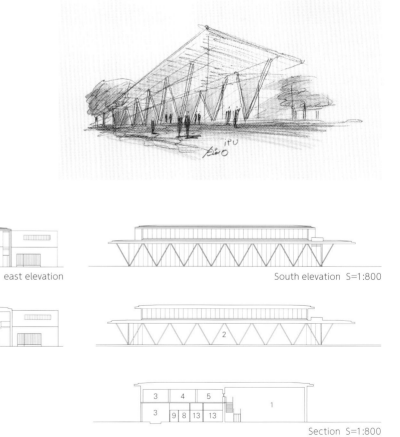

east elevation

South elevation　S=1:800

Section　S=1:800

View toward east from track. *PHILOSOPHIA* inmost　走路より東を見る。奥に［PHILOSOPHIA］

Training room: track on left　トレーニング室。左に走路

Training room　トレーニング室

View toward training room from track　走路よりトレーニング室を見る

The site is located in the western Shizuoka Prefecture, on a hill overlooking the Tenryu River at the corner of an industrial district. This factory of Rock Field, a delicatessen manufacturer in Kobe, was built during a period over 30 years in four phases, from Phase I in 1991, to phase IV in 2020.

I became acquainted with Mr. Kozo Iwata, the founder of the company, in the early 1970s when I designed *the Rose Garden* in Kobe. Mr. Iwata was one of the tenants of the building. Our close friendship began after a small quarrel over a design of the shop-sign. Advocating "education for food" as its slogan, the company grew significantly over the period of 20 years starting from the 1970s. By the end of the 1980s, he asked to design *the*

Rock Field Shizuoka Factory, which was a plan to take the company to the next level. Mr. Iwata quoted, "Above all, I want it to be a place where workers can spend their time comfortably." Following his words, the factory was arranged to integrate with the surrounding nature, and the space for employee cafeteria was designed with the most scenic view.

As the scale of the company has enlarged, Mr. Iwata's consciousness has shifted toward the creation of a comprehensive system that begins from the production site of ingredients, the fields. We have received another commission in 2003 to design the Kobe head office and factory. For this project, the challenge was to recycle architecture by renovating

PHASE I 1989-91

PHASE II 1998-2000

PHASE III 2008-09

PHASE IV 2019-20

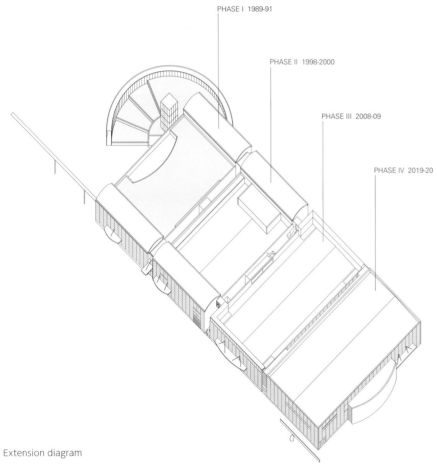

Extension diagram

Phase I

Phase II

Phase III

Rock Field Shizuoka Factory
ロック・フィールド静岡ファクトリー

Iwata, Shizuoka
静岡県磐田市
1989-2020

Overall view from west　西より見る全景

a former logistics warehouse that was damaged in the Great Hanshin-Awaji Earthquake in 1995.

In the summer of 2020, the fourth phase of the *Shizuoka Factory* project was completed. This was a drastic investment to pave the new path for the company during a turbulent social environment. In addition to an attempt to increase its production capacity and efficiency, the company took on the challenge of going one step further while maintaining its existing concepts of utilizing natural energy, a recycling-oriented production system, and a factory that integrates into the greenery as a park.

From Rock Field, every autumn we receive Jiro Persimmons as a gift. They are sent from the employees who planted many on the premises when *the Shizuoka Factory* was completed. Although the harvest was poor in the first few years, now the persimmons look and taste one of the best in the nation. Each and every seed is a symbol of the company's spirit of environmental creation.

View from southeast　南東より見る全景

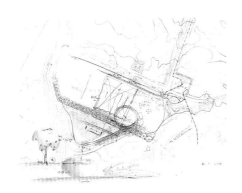

敷地は静岡県の西部, 天竜川を望む高台の工業団地の一角に位置する。1991年完成の第Ⅰ期から2020年完成の第Ⅳ期まで30年越し, 4期にわたり建設された, 神戸発の総菜メーカー, ロック・フィールドの工場施設の計画である。

創業者である岩田さんとは, 1970年代初め, 北野町の「ローズ・ガーデン」をつくった時に, 設計者と建物のテナントという形で出会った。店舗の看板のデザインで揉めたのをきっかけに, 親しい友人関係が始まった。その後, 約20年の間に, 岩田さんの会社は〈食育〉をキーワードに大きく成長した。そして, 80年代の終わり, 次なるステージへと向かうべく企画された「ロック・フィールド静岡工場」の設計依頼を受けることとなった。「何よりも働く人が気持ちよく時間を過ごせる場所にしてほしい」。常に最前線で, 自ら現場に立ってきた岩田さんらしい, この言葉を頼りに, 周囲の自然と一体化する工場を設計し, 一番見晴らしのいい空間を従業員の食堂とした。

以来, 会社の発展に合わせ, 増築を重ねてきた。規模の拡大とともに, 岩田さんの意識は, 素材の生産現場, 畑から始まる総合的な体制づくりへと向かっていく。第Ⅱ期では, 風力発電を取り入れ排水処理施設に活用, その水を循環させるビオトープなどランドスケープも整え, ファクトリー・パークのコンセプトが生まれた。さらには既存の研修センターを改造して, 従業員のための託児所も開設。企業活動全体を視野に入れた, 広い意味での, 文字通りの環境づくりが, 一歩一歩, 地道に進められてきた。2003年には, 神戸本社, 工場の設計依頼を受け, ここでは, 1995年の阪神淡路大震災で被害を受けた元物流倉庫のリノベーションによる, 文字通りのリサイクル建築に挑戦している。

そして2020年夏,「静岡ファクトリー」第Ⅳ期工事が完成を迎えた。激動する社会環境の

Wind turbines and factory: phase III on right, IV on left, linkway on top of phase III is constructed on phase IV
風力発電機とファクトリー：右がⅢ期, 左がⅣ期。Ⅲ期最上階の連絡通路はⅣ期工事

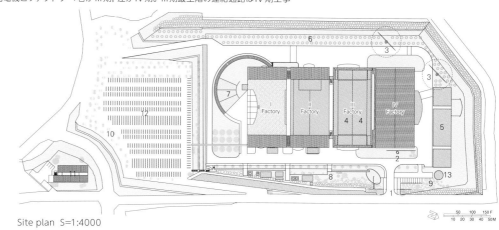

Site plan S=1:4000

1 MAIN GATE	6 PERSIMMON TREE (JIRO-GAKI)	11 NURSERY
2 POTATO SCULPTURE	7 HERB GARDEN	12 PARKING
3 WIND TURBINE	8 BIOTOPE	13 W.C.
4 PHOTOVOLTAIC GENERATING UNIT	9 MAGNOLIA GARDEN	
5 WASTEWATER TREATMENT	10 CHERRY TREES	

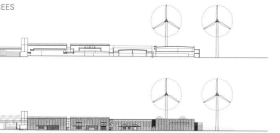

Section

West elevation S=1:4000

中で同社が次なる道を切り拓くべく, 思い切った投資であった。生産能力の増強, 効率化と共に, 自然エネルギーの活用, 循環型の生産システム, 緑に溶け込む「パーク」としての工場といった従来のコンセプトを踏襲, さらにもう一歩先に推し進めるべく挑んだ。

ロック・フィールドからの毎秋の贈り物は, 次

郎柿である。「静岡工場」完成時, 場内に従業員の数だけ植えられたもので, 彼ら自身の手で育て, 送り出される。最初の数年は実りも悪かったが, 今では見た目も味も一級品だ。この一玉一玉が, この企業の環境づくりの精神を象徴している。

View from biotope toward factory (phase IV)　ビオトープよりファクトリー (第IV期) を見る△

▽ View of factory from northwest　北西よりファクトリーを見る

View toward factory (phase I) through colonnade　コロネード越しにファクトリー (第I期)を見る

Colonnade and harb garden　コロネードとハーブガーデン

Colonnade to entrance　エントランスへ導くコロネード

Plaza of factory (phase I)　ファクトリー（第I期）の広場

Cafeteria　社員食堂

155

TADAO ANDO RECENT PROJECT 3
LIST OF PROJECTS

BOURSE DE COMMERCE / PINAULT COLLECTION
Paris, France
Design: 2016.01.-17.04.
Construction: 2017.05.-21.01.
Program: museum
Client: Collection Pinault Paris
Architect: Tadao Ando Architect & Associates—
Tadao Ando, Kazuya Okano, Hironobu Wakayama,
L'agence NeM / Niney et Marca Architectes
Local Architect: Agence Pierre-Antoine Gatier, archi-
tect en chef des monuments historiques; Setec Bati-
ment, atructural; Ronan and Erwan Bouroullec, furni-
ture & restaurant interior
Consultant: TESS engineering cupola
—Benoit Stehelin, Rubis Trinh
General contractor: Bouygues Rénovation Privée
Structural system: reinforced concrete, steel frame
Size: 3 basement, 4 stories
Site area: 3,537.5 m²
Built area: 3,537.5 m²
Total area: 9,985.9 m²
P.018 -

KRÖLLER-MÜLLER MUSEUM
Otterlo, The Netherlands
Design: 2018.01.-
Program: museum
Client: Kröller-Müller Museum
Architect: Tadao Ando Architect & Associates—
Tadao Ando, Masataka Yano, Kazutoshi Miyamura,
Hiroki Nakadoi, Ken Farris, Shogo Soga
Consultant: Toornend Partners
Structural system: reinforced concrete
Size: 2 basement, 1 stories
Site area: 371,040 m²
Built area: 15,211 m²
Total area: 32,996 m²
P. 044 -

NAKANOSHIMA CHILDREN'S BOOK FOREST
Osaka, Osaka
Design: 2017.02.-18.11.
Construction: 2018.01.-19.12.
Program: library
Client: City of Osaka
Architect: Tadao Ando Architect & Associates—
Tadao Ando, Hironobu Wakayama, Yosuke Sato
Consultant: Ascolal Structural Design Office, struc-
tural; Stech, m/e/p; Ataka Bosai Sekkei, disaster pre-
vention; BACH, book curation and display;
Rhizomatiks, video production
General contractor: Takenaka Corporation
Structural system: reinforced concrete
Size: 3 stories
Site area: 1,380.46 m²
Built area: 489.35 m²
Total area: 815.10 m²
P.052 -

WRIGHTWOOD 659
Chicago, U.S.A.
Design: 2013.06.-15.05.
Construction: 2014.09.-18.05.
Program: museum
Client: CFAB—Fred Eychaner, Daniel J. Whittaker
Architect: Tadao Ando Architect & Associates—
Tadao Ando, Masataka Yano, Kazutoshi Miyamura
Local Architect: Vinci | Hamp Architects, Gensler
Consultant: Thornton Tomasetti, structural; AEI, m/e/p
General contractor: Norcon
Structural system: brick (existing building), steel
frame, steel framed reinforced concrete
Size: 1 basement, 4 stories
Site area: 945.7 m²
Built area: 721.0 m²
Total area: 3,455.9 m²
P.072 -

TAIZO KURODA GALLERY
Ito, Shizuoka
Design: 2018.10.-19.06.
Construction: 2019.06.-20.01.
Program: art gallery
Client: TAIZO Co.
Architect: Tadao Ando Architect & Associates—
Tadao Ando, Takaaki Mizutani
General contractor: Tabata Kensetsu
Structural system: wood
Size: 1 story
Site area: 1,352.4 m²
Built area: 37.0 m²
Total area: 17.3 m²
P.088 -

LG ART CENTER
Gangseo-gu, Seoul, Korea
Design: 2015.11.-19.04.
Construction: 2019.05.-22.03. (est.)
Program: art center
Client: LG Consortium
Architect: Tadao Ando Architect & Associates—
Tadao Ando, Kazuya Okano
Local Architect: Gansam Architects & Partners., Co.,
Ltd, SKM Architects
Consultant: Theater Projects, theater
General contractor: GSE&C/Seoul
Size: 3 basement, 5 stories
Site area: 15,153 m²
Built area: 10,597.8 m²
Total area: 41,535.7 m²
P.100 -

PENTHOUSE IN MANHATTAN III
New York, U.S.A.
Design: 2013.09.-15.03.
Construction: 2014.06.-19.08.
Program: residence
Architect: Tadao Ando Architect & Associates—
Tadao Ando, Masataka Yano, Hideaki Iida
Local Architect: Toshihiro Oki Architect P.C.; Patrick
Branc, green wall artist; Eckersley O' Callaghan &
Partners, LLC, structural, glass engineer; Cosentini
Associates, m/e/p
Contractor: Caliper, stairs, metal; Vitrocsa, glass slide
door; Dinesen, floaring; AMG Glasstechnik, handrail
Structural system: steel frame, brick
Size: 1 basement, 12 stories
  (exiting building was built in 1912.)
Site area: 775 m²
Total area: 235 m² (6,840 m², exiting building)
P.106 -

HE ART MUSEUM
Foshan, Guangdong, China
Design: 2014.04.-17.02.
Construction: 2017.02.-20.10.
Program: museum
Client: INFORE HOLDING
Architect: Tadao Ando Architect & Associates—
Tadao Ando, Masataka Yano, Shimao Mori,
Kazutoshi Miyamura, Manabu Yamaya
Consultant: Beijing CCI architectural design Co., Ltd.,
structural/mechanical/landscape; Beijing Qingshang
Architectural Ornamental Engineering Co., Ltd., inte-
rior
General contractor: China State Construction Engi-
neering Co., Ltd
Structural system: reinforced concrete
Size: 2 basement, 4 stories
Site area: 8,650.5 m²
Built area: 2,780.0 m²
Total area: 16,340.0 m²
P.118 -

PROJECTS IN IPU (INTERNATIONAL PACIFIC UNIVERSITY)
Okayama, Okayama
Program: university facility
Client: Hiroshi Ohashi
  (President, Soshi Gakuen Incorporated)

"DISCOVERY"
Design: 2014.09.-17.10.
Construction: 2017.10.-19.01.
Architect: Tadao Ando Architect & Associates—
Tadao Ando, Fumihiko Iwama, Kazutoshi Miyamura,
Hiroki Nakadoi, Manabu Yamaya
General contractor: Kajima Corporation Chugoku
Branch
Structural system: steel frame
Size: 2 stories
Site area: 7,622.97 m²
Built area: 3,386.59 m²
Total area: 4,587.13 m²

"HARMONY"
Design: 2015.01.-15.09.
Construction: 2015.09.-16.03.
Architect: Tadao Ando Architect & Associates—
Tadao Ando, Fumihiko Iwama, Kazutoshi Miyamura,
Hiroki Nakadoi, Manabu Yamaya
General contractor: Kajima Corporation Chugoku
Branch
Structural system: steel frame
Size: 2 stories
Site area: 61,856.38 m²
Built area: 1,173.26 m²
Total area: 1,399.19 m²

"INSPIRE"
Design: 2017.06.-18.04.
Construction: 2018.04.-18.11.
Architect: Tadao Ando Architect & Associates—
Tadao Ando, Fumihiko Iwama, Kazutoshi Miyamura,
Hiroki Nakadoi, Manabu Yamaya
General contractor: Kajima Corporation Chugoku
Branch
Structural system: steel frame
Size: 2 stories
Site area: 2,382.13 m²
Built area: 974.84 m²
Total area: 1,181.13 m²
P.130 -

ROCK FIELD SHIZUOKA FACTORY (PHAZE IV)
Iwata, Shizuoka
Design: 2017.07.-18.12.
Construction: 2019.03.-20.09.
Program: factory
Client: ROCK FIELD
Architect: Tadao Ando Architect & Associates—
Tadao Ando, Kazuya Okano
Consultants: Ascolal Structural Design Office—
Naoto Kashimoto, Sota Katagi, structural
General contractor: Shimizu Corporation Nagoya
Branch—Daisuke Sasaki, Masahisa Ueda,
Koji Sawada, building construction; K.S. Planning
Co.—Keisuke Suzuki, Hideo Sagisaka, equipment
construction
Structural system: steel frame
Size: 3 stories
Site area: 72,842.76 m²
Built area: 4,166.07 m² (17,961.26 m², total building)
Total area: 8,214.69 m² (27,462.57 m², total building)
P.148 -

Tadao Ando
安藤忠雄

Born 1941 in Osaka, Japan. Self-educated in architecture. Established Tadao Ando Architect & Associates in 1969.

Major works include Rokko Housing, Church of the Light, FABRICA (Benetton Communications Research Center), Pulitzer Arts Foundation, Modern Art Museum of Fort Worth, Chichu Art Museum, Omotesando Hills (Omotesando Regeneration Project), Punta della Dogana Contemporary Art Centre, Shanghai Poly Theater, Clark Center / Clark Art Institute, Hill of the Buddha, Nakanoshima Children's Book Forest, He Art Museum, and Bourse de Commerce / Pinault Collection.

Awarded the Architectural Institute of Japan (AIJ) Prize for the Row House in Sumiyoshi in 1979, Japan Art Academy Prize in 1993, Pritzker Architecture Prize in 1995, Person of Cultural Merit (Japan) in 2003, International Union of Architects (UIA) Gold Medal in 2005, John F. Kennedy Center Gold Medal in the Arts in 2010, Shimpei Goto Award in 2010, Order of Culture (Japan) in 2010, Commander of the Order of Art and Letters (France) in 2013, Grand Officer of the Order of Merit (Italy) in 2015, and Isamu Noguchi Award in 2016. Held solo exhibitions at the Museum of Modern Art (MoMA) in 1991 and Centre Pompidou in 1993.

Vice Chairman of The Reconstruction Design Council in Response to the Great East Japan Earthquake, 2011. Committee Chairman of Momo-Kaki Orphans Fund, Great East Japan Earthquake.

Taught as a visiting professor at Yale University, Columbia University, and Harvard University. Professor at the University of Tokyo from 1997. Professor emeritus of the University of Tokyo since 2003.

大阪生まれ。独学で建築を学び、1969年に安藤忠雄建築研究所を設立。

代表作に「六甲の集合住宅」、「光の教会」、「FABRICA (ベネトンアートスクール)」、「ピューリッツァー美術館」、「フォートワース現代美術館」、「地中美術館」、「表参道ヒルズ(同潤会青山アパート建替計画)」、「プンタ・デラ・ドガーナ」、「上海保利大劇場」、「クラーク美術館」、「真駒内滝野霊園 頭大仏」、「兵庫県立美術館増築棟 Ando Gallery」、「こども本の森 中之島」、「和美術館」、「ブルス・ドゥ・コメルス／ピノー・コレクション」など。

1979年「住吉の長屋」で日本建築学会賞、85年アルヴァ・アアルト賞、89年フランス建築アカデミーゴールドメダル、93年日本芸術院賞、95年朝日賞、95年プリツカー賞、96年高松宮殿下記念世界文化賞、02年AIAゴールドメダル、京都賞、03年文化功労者、05年UIA(国際建築家連合)ゴールドメダル、レジオンドヌール勲章(シュヴァリエ)、06年環境保全功労者。10年ジョン・F・ケネディーセンター芸術金賞、後藤新平賞、文化勲章。12年リチャード・ノイトラ賞、13年フランス芸術文化勲章(コマンドゥール)、15年イタリアの星勲章(グランデ・ウフィチャーレ章)、16年イサム・ノグチ賞。21年レジオン・ドヌール勲章(コマンドゥール)叙勲。

2011年東日本大震災復興構想会議議長代理、「桃・柿育英会 東日本大震災遺児育英資金」実行委員長。

イェール、コロンビア、ハーヴァード大学の客員教授歴任。1997年より東京大学教授、2003年より名誉教授。

STAFF
Tadao Ando Architect & Associates
安藤忠雄建築研究所

Tadao Ando	安藤忠雄
Masataka Yano	矢野正隆
Fumihiko Iwama	岩間文彦
Kazuya Okano	岡野一也
Takaaki Mizutani	水谷孝明
Hironobu Wakayama	若山泰伸
Kanya Sogo	十河完也
Yoshinori Hayashi	林慶憲
Shimao Mori	森詩麻夫
Kazutoshi Miyamura	宮村和寿
Junpei Fukuda	福田純平
Yosuke Sato	佐藤洋輔
Shogo Soga	曽我章悟
Yuya Goto	後藤裕也
Takafumi Hiramatsu	平松崇史
Chisato Kodaira	古平知沙都
Akiko Hayashida	林田安紀子
Yume Kajiwara	梶原夢
Saki Takahashi	髙橋沙季
Tamao Shichiri	七里玉緒
Hisae Sato	佐藤久恵
Yumiko K. Ando	安藤由美子

Cover:
Bourse de Commerce / Pinault Collection
Title page:
Nakanoshima Children's Book Forest
——

English translation:
Fraze Craze Inc.: pp.8-17／Ikuko Emi: p.106, pp.120-121
——

Credits:
Photographs
GA photographers: p.158
p.10, p.11, Yukio Futagawa／pp.18-43, pp.52-63, pp.66-70, pp.72-99, pp.110-115, pp.130-155, Yoshio Futagawa／
p.9 below, Yoshio Takase

pp.14-15, p.36 below: Philippe Guignard Air Images
Courtesy Bourse de Commerce – Pinault Collection. ©Tadao Ando Architect & Associates, NeM / Niney et Marca
Architectes, Agence Pierre-Antoine Gatier.
p.46 top of right: Jannes Linders
p.46 second and third from right top: Marjon Gemmeke Collection Kröller-Müller Museum, Otterlo, the Netherlands
p.107, pp.116-117: Jeff Goldberg / Esto
pp.118-119, p.122, pp.124-125 above, p.125 above, p.128: ©HEM
p.129: Liu Xiangli ©HEM
p.123, pp.126-127: Tian Fangfang
p.124 below: Tian Fangfang ©One-Tenth Art Company
pp.44-45, p.65, p.70 right top and bottom, p.71, p.100, p.102 above, p.103 below, p.148 below:
Courtesy of Tadao Ando Architect & Associates

Drawings
p.46 fourth to sixth from right top: Collection Kröller-Müller Museum, Otterlo, the Netherlands
Sketches, Hand Drawings, Renderings and Architectural Drawings:
Tadao Ando Architect & Associates

TADAO ANDO RECENT PROJECT 3
安藤忠雄 最新プロジェクト3

2021年9月24日発行

企画：二川由夫
撮影：GA photographers
印刷・製本：シナノ印刷株式会社
制作・発行：エーディーエー・エディタ・トーキョー
151-0051 東京都渋谷区千駄ヶ谷3-12-14
TEL.(03)3403-1581(代)

ISBN 978-4-87140-693-2 C1052